THE COMPROMISING OF AMERICA

An American Tragedy

RICHARD MCKENZIE NEAL

authorHOUSE®

AuthorHouse™
1663 Liberty Drive
Bloomington, IN 47403
www.authorhouse.com
Phone: 1-800-839-8640

First published by AuthorHouse 9/22/2011

ISBN: 978-1-4670-3741-9 (e)
ISBN: 978-1-4670-3742-6 (hc)
ISBN: 978-1-4670-3743-3 (sc)

Library of Congress Control Number: 2011916870

Printed in the United States of America

FOREWORD

I've heard it said that while you can ignore reality, you cannot ignore the consequences of ignoring reality.

I've also heard it said that perspective is reality for the unengaged individual, and we can apply that notion to a large segment of our population. But the real reality is that our country is speeding toward a financial train wreck...even as we're picking up speed. A basic rule of thumb for Financial Stability 101 is that one doesn't spend more than one earns, but recent generations... and this administration have lost touch with that reality also.

We're currently living in a fantasy world of smoke and mirrors where almost one-half of our population is receiving some level of unearned welfare, financial assistance and/or various other "entitlement" benefits. The number of beneficiaries has not only grown steadily over the generations, but has now reached a point where it has become a way of life...the norm. They expect our government to take care of them from the cradle to the grave. With their large numbers and voting block, their congressional representatives will do whatever it takes to keep them happy and voting status quo. As long as they can vote themselves more and more of the working class' money, they can continue ignoring reality.

We've all either said or heard that if we could take all the "special interest" groups out of Washington, we could get some real unbiased reform done on cleaning up the mess we currently have in Congress. Well, guess what? Government is its own special interest group...the biggest special interest group of all. With no term limits members become so entrenched, by catering to "their" special interest groups, that their reelections are almost guaranteed each reelection cycle. The situation points to an institutional problem for Congress, "the arguably narcissistic attitude that longer is better."

Government is now only the stooge perpetuating Ponzi economics. Wars are being waged to support the scheme and there's a gun pointed at the heads of world leaders to ensure they stay engaged. It is now job creation and economic growth at all costs, when jobs and economic growth are the problems, not the solution. Ponzi credit has created too many jobs. And most of those jobs have nothing to do with individuals making a living or creating tangibles.

This planet no longer has government. It has disablement. It has Ponzi salesmen. The global Ponzi credit system is the greatest crime against humanity ever perpetrated. It has squandered the planet's resources and institutionalized un-sustainability. It has created money flow, control and power that make their way into the hands of the undeserving. It has created a global frenzy for profit.

Humanity had almost defeated all its predation, competition and disease, only to find itself competing and preyed upon by the worst competition imaginable...itself. It has institutionalized necessity for economic growth and population increase when the planet cannot sustain it. The game controllers are poised to profit from dwindling resources through commodity investment and war. We are forced to play a real-life monopoly game with cheaters who change the rules. The world's jobs are dependent on the continuation of Ponzi credit creation.

Global warming is government's latest political catch-phrase (still questioned by many) to create new green jobs and save the planet; I would suggest that perhaps we should be looking into some type of population control. The world cannot continue to support unlimited population growth...but of course, that wouldn't fly in today's politically correct world. Population constraints would also be very beneficial in our ever-ballooning government sponsored welfare and entitlement programs.

Do you really think when the "Banking Consortium" got together with government to institutionalize private money creation, that they really invented a benevolent sustainable pyramid scheme? Government was duped by the enticement of making its job easier while entrenching unaccountability. This disablement is now complete. By trying to make its job easier, it made its job impossible. We don't have government and humanity is losing the meaning of governance.

But getting back to reality, who's to say where A New World Order will take us? It's already becoming gray and abstract even as we're being herded in the direction of secularism. The younger generation(s) appear oblivious to how fast the world is changing, but more importantly... and without historical perspective, they're unaware of the sharp left turn we negotiated back in 2008.

It's almost as though we've become non-entities, indistinguishable components in this New World Order that's heedlessly moving ahead...with or without our buy in.

Just look around at our recent younger generations. They're like zombies...moving about with their heads down, texting and/or constantly double-checking their cells to make sure they haven't missed a text in the last minute or two. They appear to have lost touch with the real world...oblivious to their surroundings. Is it that they can't deal with being alone or independent of their techno support circle that keeps them in a mode of constant preoccupation with a non-judgmental keypad? Are they driven by insecurities that need ongoing approval and validation from their contemporaries?

Maybe, but conceivably it's much bigger, perhaps it's a worldwide transformation to level mankind's playing field...to create a uniform world where everyone is equal. Ultimately, the stated goal of this administration is to redistribute the wealth and we're certainly seeing his relentless push to bring America down to the levels of the less prosperous countries. It seems that everything American is now being manufactured in other countries around the world, even as our unemployment numbers remain unacceptable. It's mind numbing to watch as we persist in digging ourselves deeper and deeper into an unforgiving abyss of debt. We currently have several states in the same, or worse financial situation as Greece and several other socialistic countries around the world. Wake-up America!

High school dropout rates have been the drivers for various government-sponsored programs like California's Truancy Response Program. We (the tax payers) pay for the extra school truancy police, juvenile court judges, administrators and counselors for this program, even as the numbers continue to climb...unabated. Now my question is: Whatever happened to parenting? As a kid growing up in Arkansas I never challenged my parent's negative reply to a request of mine. If their answer was "No," I may not have liked it...but I knew not to pursue the subject matter further. I would also suggest that, in a free society, there never should have been such a program. How is it that expensive programs that aspire, with limited success, to overcome the failures of some parents, should be financed by those parents who take personal responsibility for their own children's school attendance?

The "dumbing" down of our government run schools where teaching "what to think" rather than "how to think," has become the accepted practice in many schools; and critical thinking has been the biggest casualty. Without critical thinking, the young and naïve will be less likely to question the well crafted and polished, political spin machine.

Reality will then, like common sense, common courtesies, accountability and responsibility...become an intangible relic from another time, another place.

And you can rest assured that the consequences will follow...

Experience is a hard teacher because she gives the test first, the lesson afterwards.

CHAPTER 1

The Fourth of July may be just a holiday for fireworks to some people. But it was a momentous day for the history of this country and the history of the world.

Not only did July 4, 1776, mark American independence from England, it marked a radically different kind of government from the governments that prevailed around the world at the time...and the kinds of governments that had prevailed for thousands of years.

It has been said that the United States is the only country founded on an idea, or a set of ideas, rather than on ethnic or racial similarities, kinship, conquest or the simple fact of a relatively homogeneous group of people living in the same geographic region for centuries. Those ideas are summed up in the Declaration of Independence, the document whose signing and promulgation we celebrate. In some ways it can lay claim to being the most revolutionary public document in human history.

Aspects of the idea that people are not just vassals of the powers that be, interchangeable cogs in the great machinery of society presided over by leaders who had by and large established themselves through conquest and pillage, had been growing for centuries before 1776. But the circumstances surrounding the decision of the Colonists to separate from Great Britain offered the opportunity to summarize emerging principles in a uniquely eloquent manner.

The American Revolution was not simply a rebellion against the king of England; it was a rebellion against being ruled by kings in general. That is why the opening salvo of the American Revolution was called "the shot heard round the world."

Autocratic rulers and their subjects heard that shot... and things that had not been questioned for millennia were now open to challenge. As the generations went by, more and more autocratic governments around the world proved unable to meet that challenge.

Some clever people today ask whether the United States has really been "exceptional." You couldn't be more exceptional in the 18th century than to create your fundamental document...the Constitution of the United States...by opening with the momentous words, "We the people."

Those three words were a slap in the face to those who thought themselves entitled to rule, and who regarded the people as if they were simply human livestock, destined to be herded and shepherded by their betters. Indeed, to this very day, elites who think that way...and that includes many among the intelligentsia, as well as political messiahs...find the Constitution of the United States a real pain because it stands in the way of their imposing their will and their presumptions on the rest of us.

More than a hundred years ago, so-called "Progressives" began a campaign to undermine the Constitution's strict limitations on government, which stood in the way of self-anointed political crusaders imposing their grand schemes on all the rest of us. That effort to discredit the Constitution continues to this day, and the arguments haven't really changed much in 100 years.

The cover story in the July 4th issue of Time magazine is a classic example of this arrogance. It asks of the Constitution: "Does it still matter?"

A long and rambling essay by Time magazine's managing editor, Richard Stengel, manages to create a toxic blend of the irrelevant and the erroneous.

The irrelevant comes first, pointing out in big letters that those who wrote the Constitution did not know about all sorts of things in the world today, including airplanes, television, computers and DNA.

This may seem like a clever new gambit but, like many clever new gambits, it is a rehash of arguments made long ago. Back in 1908, Woodrow Wilson said, "When the Constitution was framed there were no railways, there was no telegraph, there was no telephone."

In Mr. Stengel's rehash of this argument, he declares: "People on the right and left constantly ask what the framers would say about some event that is happening today."

Maybe that kind of talk goes on where he hangs out. But most people have enough common sense to know that a constitution does not exist to micromanage particular events or express opinions about the passing scene.

A constitution exists to create a framework for govern-ment...and the Constitution of the United States tries to keep the government inside that framework.

From the irrelevant to the erroneous is a short step for

Mr. Stengel. He says, "If the Constitution was intended to limit the federal government, it certainly doesn't say so."

Apparently Mr. Stengel has not read the 10th Amendment: "The powers not delegated to the United States by the Constitution, nor prohibited by it to the States, are reserved to the States respectively, or to the people."

Perhaps Richard Stengel should follow the advice of another Stengel...Casey Stengel, who said on a number of occasions, "You could look it up."

More than 200 years later, the shining city on the hill has lost much of its sheen. Government has expanded into all manner of individual freedoms. Government holds a gun to your head and compels you to buy its retirement plan upon pain of your job. This retirement plan is a giant Ponzi scheme beyond the reach of the courts. Now comes a government health care plan that compels you to buy health insurance upon pain of injurious levy at the hands of the IRS. President George Washington would have donned his uniform and called up the militia upon hearing this news, were he alive today.

We the people have been poor stewards of the founders' grand idea. Our schools no longer teach the founders' dream, and new generations are even more foggy and uncaring about what shook the Earth more than 200 years ago in Philadelphia. If we do not teach the founders' dream in our schools, we cannot expect our progeny to know or care, and, without that, we are doomed.

We now resemble an aging European country, layered with government entitlements and government rules and regulations that keep mounting without end. Today America's national character and "exceptionalism" are in damager of disappearing within our intrusive and ever expanding government. American "exceptionalism" has always been about our creative and inventive genius fueled by free markets, our belief that diversity gives us strength, our special personal kindness and caring for others at home and beyond our shores and our belief in the power and glory of the individual as the light of liberty.

Can we recover our past and once again be that beacon of individual liberty on Earth? We could do it, but it would take a wholesale reordering of our governments across the land and changes in our schools that would be fiercely resisted by powerful forces. I'm doubtful we have the mettle to deal with all of that. And as I look around, I can't say history is on our side.

We, in the United States, have been blessed to live in a nation founded on a principle that is unique to government throughout all of human history...the right to life, liberty and the pursuit of happiness.

In the Middle East today, we see great unrest because people are unhappy with government. They want freedom and a government that provides the rights and opportunities that we have in the United States, which we now largely take for granted.

But we are slowly losing our rights as government at the federal, state and local levels increasingly become more intrusive. Too many today fail to realize just how superb this nation's founding documents are. Life should not first be about how to make a good living; life should first be about being a good citizen, to respect and honor the founders of this nation and understand and defend the government they created.

The writers of the Declaration of Independence were faced with the challenging task of justifying their rebellion against King George III and the government of England to which they had been subjected to for generations. This justification forced them "first" to embrace the principles of God, and then...man and government, which they called "self-evident" truths. The most pivotal of these was their declaration that the rights of men are derived not from the government, but from "their creator." As such, there were limits on what any earthly government could do.

Today we are faced with a powerful movement to deny this basis for our rights. Instead of "unalienable rights" we have "civil rights" originating from civil government rather than God. The government has become God in the minds of those constituting the government, and there are no longer any limits on what it can do to us.

Does the Constitution matter? If it doesn't, then your freedom doesn't matter.

CHAPTER 2

Recently the media has been so preoccupied with a Congressman's photograph of himself in his underwear that there has been scant attention paid to the fact that Iran continues advancing toward creating a nuclear bomb, and nobody is doing anything that is likely to stop them.

Nuclear weapons in the hands of the world's leading sponsor of international terrorism might seem to be something that would sober up even the most giddy members of the chattering class. But that chilling prospect cannot seem to compete for attention with cheap behavior by an immature Congressman, infatuated with himself.

A society that cannot or will not focus on matters of life and death is a society whose survival as a free nation is at least, questionable. As hard as it may be to conceive, the world we have grown used to, and taken for granted... could come to an end, and it could happen in the lifetime of today's generation.

Those who founded the United States of America were keenly aware that they were making a radical departure from the kinds of governments under which human beings had lived over the centuries...and that this new government's success was by no means guaranteed. Monarchies in Europe had lasted for centuries and the Chinese dynasties for thousands of years. But a democratic republic was something else.

While the convention that was writing the Constitution of the United States was still in session, a lady asked Benjamin Franklin what the delegation was creating. He replied, "A republic, madam...if you can keep it."

In the middle of the next century, Abraham Lincoln still posed it as a question whether "government of the people, by the people and for the people shall not perish from the earth." Years earlier, Lincoln had warned of the dangers to a free society from its own designing power-seekers... and how only the vigilance, wisdom and dedication of the public could preserve their freedom.

But today, few people seem to see such dangers, either internally or internationally.

A recent poll showed that nearly half the American public believes that the government should redistribute wealth. That so many people are so willing to blithely put such an enormous and dangerous arbitrary power in the hands of politicians...risking their own freedom, in hopes of getting what someone else has...is a painful sign of how far many citizens and voters fall short of what is needed to preserve a democratic republic.

The ease with which people with wealth can ship it overseas electronically, or put it in tax shelters at home, means that raising the tax rate on wealthy people is not going to bring in the kind of tax revenue that would enable wealth redistribution to provide the bonanza that some people are expecting.

In other words, people who are willing to give government more arbitrary power can give up their birthright of freedom without even getting the mess of pottage. Worse yet, they can give up their children's and their grandchildren's birthright of freedom.

Free and democratic societies have existed for a relatively short time, as history is measured...and their staying power has always been open to question. So much depends on the wisdom of the voters that the franchise was always limited, in one way or another, so that voting would be confined to those with a stake in the viability and progress of the country, and the knowledge to cast their vote intelligently.

In our own times, however, voting has been seen as just one of the many "rights" to which everyone is supposed to be entitled. The emphasis has been on the voter, rather than on the momentous consequences of elections for the nation today and for generations yet unborn.

To those who see voting as more or less just a matter of self-expression, almost a recreational activity, there is no need to inform themselves on both sides of the issues before voting, much less sit down and think beyond the rhetoric to the realities that the rhetoric conceals.

Careless voters may be easily swayed by charisma and rhetoric, oblivious to the monumental disasters created around the world by 20th century leaders with charisma and rhetoric, such as Hitler.

Voters like this represent a danger of terminal frivolity for freedom and our Republic.

Hearing politicians, national and international talking heads and pseudo-academics praising the Middle East stirrings as "democracy movements" is truly disgusting to me. We also hear democracy as the description of our own political system, but like the founders of our nation, I find democracy and majority rule a contemptible form of government.

I'll begin by quoting one of our founders on the subject of democracy: James Madison, in Federalist Paper No. 10, wrote: "In a pure democracy, there is nothing to check the inducement to sacrifice the weaker party or the obnoxious individual."

> At the 1787 Constitution Convention, Virginia Governor Edmund Randolph said, "That in tracking these evils to their origin, every man had found it in the turbulence and follies of democracy."

> John Adams said, "Remember, democracy never lasts long. It soon wastes, exhausts and murders itself. There was never a democracy yet that did not commit suicide."

> Alexander Hamilton said, "We are now forming a Republican form of government. Real liberty is not found in the extremes of democracy, but in moderate governments. If we incline too much to democracy, we shall soon shoot into a monarchy or some other form of dictatorship."

The word "democracy" appears nowhere in the two most fundamental documents of our nation...the Declaration of Independence nor the Constitution. If you don't want to bother reading our founding documents, just ask yourself: Does our Pledge of Allegiance to the flag say to "the democracy for which it stands," or to "the Republic for which it stands?" Or perhaps Julia Ward Howe made a mistake in titling her Civil War song "The Battle Hymn of the Republic?" What's the difference between republican and democratic forms of government? John Adams captured the essence: "You have rights antecedent to all earthly governments; rights that cannot be repealed or restrained by human laws; rights derived from the Great Legislator of the Universe." That means Congress does not grant us rights; their job is to protect our natural or God-given rights.

The First Amendment doesn't say Congress shall grant us freedom of speech, the press and religion. It says, "Congress shall make no law respecting an establishment of religion, or prohibiting the free exercise thereof; or abridging the freedom of speech, or of the press."

Contrast the framers' vision of a republic with that of a democracy: Webster defines a democracy as "government by the people; especially: rule of the majority." In a democracy, the majority rules either directly or through its elected representatives. As in a "monarchy," the law is whatever the government determines it to be. Laws do not represent reason. They represent force. The restraint is upon the individual instead of government. Unlike that envisioned under a republican form of government, rights are seen as privileges and permissions that are granted by, and can be rescinded by, government.

With this administration, the characteristics of a monarchy are surfacing routinely...and with just a matter of fact delivery. And of course, we already have King Obama and his Queen.

To highlight the offensiveness to liberty that democracy and majority rule is, just ask yourself how many decisions in your life would you like to be made democratically. How about what car you drive, where you live, whom you marry, whether you have turkey or ham for Thanksgiving? If those decisions were made through a democratic process, the average person would see it as tyranny. Is it no less tyranny for the democratic process to determine whether you purchase health insurance or save for retirement?

Both for ourselves, and our fellow man around the globe, we should be advocating liberty, not the democracy that we've become.

CHAPTER 3

A dam Smith (1723-1790) is the father of modern economics. In 1776, he published "The Wealth of Nations," the most influential work on economics ever published. It provided a foundation for capitalism, and it transformed economic thought. The first edition sold out in six months, and the book went through four more editions in Smith's lifetime.

Smith pointed out the flaws of mercantilism, which prescribed heavy government regulation of the economy, and high tariffs. Smith showed the benefits of a free enterprise system, in which each individual works for his own profit. To maximize profit, he must offer a better product or sell his product at a lower price than his competitor.

As Smith wrote, "It is not from the benevolence of the butcher, the brewer or the baker that we expect our dinner, but from their regard to their own interest." In other words, each is pursuing his profit, and has no intention of benefiting society, which is still the driver.

The Pilgrims, more than a century earlier, learned this lesson the hard way. They initially farmed their land communally. All shared in providing the labor, and all shared in the crops. The result? They went hungry. Half of them died the first year.

After a couple of years, they divided the land into individual plots, and each family farmed its own land. Production soared. They never starved again.

As Adam Smith observed, people respond to incentives. Give them the incentive to be productive, and they will be. Take away the profit motive, and the result is predictable.

Societies will benefit, and a higher standard of living will result. Smith's momentous work coincided with the beginning of the Industrial Revolution. His economic principles, combined with the inventiveness of people responding to the profit motive, have produced the longest period of sustained economic growth in human history.

Is there any role for government? Adam Smith would say a limited role. It would provide for a few social needs that could not be met by the free market. It would prevent monopolies, defend the nation and operate a court system to ensure the rule of law and that contracts are enforced.

Interestingly, Smith, a Scot, also had an interest in our Revolution. He argued that Britain should let go of the American colonies, which it fettered with harsh economic regulations, requiring that they import products only from British merchants.

Smith applied an economic cost-benefit analysis to Britain's overseas policies and found that the benefits to its merchants were far outweighed by the costs.

Perhaps we should apply his sagacity to both our finances and our foreign policy.

A great empire was established for the sole purpose of rising up a nation of customers who should be obliged to buy from the shops of their local producers, all the goods with which those producers could supply them. For the sake of a little enhancement of price that this monopoly might afford these producers, the consumers have been burdened with the expense of maintaining and defending this empire.

We have, over the past several lifetimes, grown accustomed to the idea that each generation is better off than the one preceding it. This is far from the norm. For thousands of years prior to 1776, it was quite common for living standards to be stagnant from one generation to the next...often staying virtually unchanged for centuries. Our past 200-plus years have been truly remarkable.

But America's exceptional run began to unravel as a creeping virus began developing within our heretofore-conservative country. The progressives first started coming out of their closets and making themselves known during the window between 1890 and 1920. Over the ensuing years progressivism's growing influence has caused our ship to take on additional baggage...and a pronounced list to the portside. The movement has been extremely subtle, almost indiscernible...but always relentlessly pervasive.

While we have historically thought of America as a conservative country, the results of a recent Gallup poll will probably come as a surprise to many. In a 2010 Gallup poll, 42 percent of Americans surveyed described themselves as conservative, 35 percent as moderate and 20 percent as liberal, percentages that have remained much the same for many, many years.

So if 42 percent of Americans are conservative, and another 35 percent are not liberal, how is it that our country's politics appear to be more liberal than conservative? Even the recent political successes of the Tea Party movement have resulted in little, if any, significant change in government policies and activities.

I suggest that most moderates, along with a goodly portion of professed conservatives, effectively support one or more liberal ideals and policies in one way or another. Witness, half of all U.S. voters in 2008 opted for an overtly non-conservative, Barack Obama. How did most moderates and a considerable number of conservatives cast such a liberal, big-government vote?

When it comes to politics, we become a double-minded-citizenry. As described in an opinion piece in this January's Christian Science Monitor: "American political opinion looks in two directions...both left and right, or liberal and conservative. At the same time, most Americans have conservative attitudes concerning the size of government and liberal beliefs in support of programs to protect themselves economically. This leads majorities to favor smaller government, individual initiative, and local control while endorsing major governmental programs ranging from Social Security to student grants and loans."

But of course, these attitudes are conflicting. Something must give, and generally it's loss of commitment to small government, individual initiative and local control...in favor of payments from federal transfer programs. As our citizenry has demonstrated, it is difficult to refuse offers of government payments, particularly when told that someone else will be footing the tab...usually, the "rich." The bottom line is that a large segment of U.S. citizens simply don't walk the talk.

There is another important reason, I would argue, that our nation's largely conservative bent yields liberal governmental policies. Many moderates, and conservatives as well, do not pause to weigh the aims and costs of government policy proposals against their professed political ideology. Perhaps they don't have a thorough understanding of which government decisions and policies are consistent with conservative ideologies.

The political cacophony is most evident among independents, many of which seem to have abandoned any cohesive political ideology in favor of picking and choosing according to the mood of the moment. Being an independent means being free to have an eclectic, frequently changing collection of political arrows. Not surprisingly, the arrows that are bowed most often are the self-serving liberal ones, regardless of one's core beliefs. A similar criticism could be levied against many conservatives, though their mix of arrows is likely to be at least somewhat more politically consistent.

Finally, the majority of voters of all persuasions tend to judge government programs by their professed social aims, with far less attention paid to the economic cost or to the realistic prospects for attaining the stated goals. In practice, the stated aims of most government programs are but partially achieved, and in some cases, the results are even counterproductive to those aims.

Most of us want to be viewed by our neighbors as good people. Moreover we also expect to get our well-deserved, fair share of the massive and rapidly growing government pie. The result is the contradictory juxtaposition of a myriad of liberal government policies endorsed (even if passively) by a largely conservative electorate.

CHAPTER 4

C all it progressivism or call it liberalism...they're both just pseudo names being utilized because the word Socialism and/or any facsimile of a system to make life fair, represents a negative connotation to the "working class." I've stated many times that life "ain't" fair, so just deal with it.

In Brief:

Progressivism is a political philosophy that takes as its objective the greatest political and economic good of the greatest number (sometimes called the common good). It is, therefore, a form of liberal populism. Progressives do not seek change merely for the sake of change, but rather insofar as the institutions and practices of a society depart from this objective and hence require reform. Progressivism thus stands in sharpest contrast to economic elitism and political authoritarianism.

The Definition of Progressivism:

Progressivism may be defined briefly as the core principles and beliefs of Progressives.

However, this definition begs the key question, since it says nothing concerning these core beliefs.

It would be better, then, to define Progressivism as the specifically American development of liberal populism that seeks social and economic justice above all else, most specifically with reference to the obstacles posed to social and economic justice by large corporations and banks. Though Progressives strongly support civil liberties, the "progress" in Progressivism lies, most fundamentally, with ensuring, as the American pledge to the flag puts it, "justice for all." Because of this core concern, Progressives have advocated governance "of the people, by the people, for the people." The phrase "the people" here stands in sharp contrast to governance by the corporation, or rather its principle owners and beneficiaries.

This definition is, however, controversial and rarely offered, probably because some Democratic politicians who wish to call themselves Progressives obtain much of their campaign financing from large corporations and also because of the pervasive influence of large corporations more generally.

Progressivism and the US Class War:

Economic elites emerge in every society and invariably seek to promote their own interests, all too often against those of taxpayers, consumers, employees, citizens, and parents. By definition, economic elites enjoy greater wealth, and therefore influence, than the ordinary citizen, and they typically attempt to exploit these advantages politically, using them as leverage to obtain still greater wealth and influence. And since the desire for wealth and power is rarely satisfied, there tend to be recurring cycles of concentrated political and economic power, together with the corruption that always attends these. One such cycle of corruption was seen in the United States around the turn of the 20th century, culminating in the economic crash of 1929. At the turn of the 21st century, the United States is in the midst of another.

Progressive Media:

The entire American broadcast media, and most of the printed media as well, are owned and administrated primarily by wealthy individuals. Direct ties to the biggest of big businesses are unbelievably extensive, and I believe these ties seriously bias and compromise news coverage, particularly coverage of economic issues. Moreover, the media empires are, first and foremost, profit-making corporations that conduct themselves like other corporations when it comes to corrupting American politics. That is, the parent corporations of many...make so-called "campaign contributions" and also act against the public interest in other ways. As big winners in the corruption game, they show no signs of serious interest in political reform. As large corporations themselves, the mass media want the same preferential treatment, and have the same desire to grow without bounds, as all other corporations.

Allegations of political bias in the media are common, although there is considerable controversy concerning the nature of this bias...as neither liberals or conservatives are pleased. Conservatives allege that the media exhibit a liberal bias. On the other hand, liberals allege that the media exhibit a pro-corporate, plutocratic bias. However, I believe such charges rely on a faulty and simplistic analysis of the American political and economic spectrum. The truth is that the apparent liberalism of some of the mass media is primarily cultural, and rarely economic. In effect, and like most other American institutions, the mass media advance the economic interests of the wealthy few at the cost of the interests, and values, of the majority; and the self-indulgent, empire-building interests of the wealthy few are not those of either liberals or cultural conservatives.

A Brief Overview of Progressive Education:

During most of the twentieth century, the term "progressive education" has been used to describe ideas and practices that aim to make schools more effective agencies of a democratic society. Although there are numerous differences of style and emphasis among progressive educators, they share the conviction that democracy means active participation by all citizens in social, political and economic decisions that will affect their lives. The education of a more engaged citizenry, according to this perspective, involves two essential elements. First: Respect for diversity, meaning that each individual should be recognized for his or her own abilities, interests, ideas, needs, and cultural identity. Secondly: The development of critical, socially engaged intelligence, which enables individuals to understand and participate effectively in the affairs of their community in a collaborative effort to achieve a common good. These elements of progressive education have been termed "child-centered" and "social reconstructionist" approaches, and while in extreme forms they have sometimes been separated, in the thoughts of John Dewey and other major theorists they are seen as being necessarily related to each other.

These progressive principles have never been the predominant philosophy in American education. From their inception in the 1830s, state systems of common or public schooling have primarily attempted to achieve cultural uniformity, not diversity, and to educate dutiful, not critical citizens. Furthermore, schooling has been under constant pressure to support the ever-expanding industrial economy by establishing a competitive meritocracy and preparing workers for their vocational roles. The term "progressive" arose from a period (roughly 1890-1920) during which many Americans took a more careful look at the political and social effects of vast concentrations of corporate power and private wealth. Dewey, in particular, saw that with the decline of local community life and small scale enterprise, young people were losing valuable opportunities to learn the arts of democratic participation, and he concluded that education would need to make up for this loss. In his Laboratory School at the University of Chicago, where he worked between 1896 and 1904, Dewey tested ideas he shared with leading school reformers such as Francis W. Parker and Ella Flagg Young. Between 1899 and 1916 he circulated his ideas in works such as The School and Society, The Child and the Curriculum, Schools of Tomorrow, and Democracy and Education, and through numerous lectures and articles. During those years other experimental schools were established around the country, and in 1919 the Progressive Education Association was founded, with the aim of "reforming the entire school system of America."

Led by Dewey, progressive educators opposed a growing national movement that sought to separate academic education for the few and narrow vocational training for the masses. During the 1920s, when education turned increasingly to "scientific" techniques such as intelligence testing and cost-benefit management, progressive educators insisted on the importance of the emotional, artistic, and creative aspects of human development... "the most living and essential parts of our natures," as Margaret Naumburg put it in her book, The Child and the World. After the Great Depression began, a group of politically oriented progressive educators, led by George Counts, dared schools to "build a new social order" and published a provocative journal called The Social Frontier to advance their "reconstructionist" critique of laissez faire capitalism. At Teachers College, Columbia University, William H. Kilpatrick and other students of Dewey taught the principles of progressive education to thousands of teachers and school leaders. In the middle part of the century, books such as Dewey's Experience and Education (1938) and several other books by Progressive educators continued to provide a progressive critique of conventional assumptions about teaching, learning and schooling. A major research endeavor, the "eight-year study," demonstrated that students from progressive high schools were capable, adaptable learners and excelled even in the finest universities.

Nevertheless, in the 1950s, during a time of cold war anxiety and cultural conservatism, progressive education was widely repudiated, and it disintegrated as an identifiable movement. However, in the years since, various groups of educators have rediscovered the ideas of Dewey and his associates, and revised them to address the changing needs of schools, children, and society in the late twentieth century. Open classrooms, schools without walls, cooperative learning, multiage approaches, whole language, the social curriculum, experiential education, and numerous forms of alternative schools all have important philosophical roots in progressive education. John Goodlad's notion of "non-graded" schools (introduced in the late 1950s), Theodore Sizer's network of "essential" schools, Elliott Wigginton's Foxfire project, and Deborah Meier's student-centered Central Park East schools are some well known examples of progressive reforms in public education; in the 1960s. Critics like Paul Goodman and George Dennison took Dewey's ideas in a more radical direction, helping give rise to the free school movement. In recent years, activist educators in inner cities have advocated greater equity, justice, diversity and other democratic values through the publication Rethinking Schools and the National Coalition of Education Activists.

Today, scholars, educators and activists are rediscovering Dewey's work and exploring its relevance to a "postmodern" age, an age of global capitalism and breathtaking cultural change, and an age in which the ecological health of the planet itself is seriously threatened. They are suggesting that although Dewey wrote a century ago, his insights into democratic culture and meaningful education suggest hopeful alternatives to the regime of standardization and mechanization that more than ever dominate our schools.

Because the curriculum is government driven, if/when teachers fail to educate our children, they don't lose one dime, no matter how much those children and the country lose by their failure. If the schools waste precious time indoctrinating children, instead of educating them, that's the children's problem and the country's problem, but not the teachers' problem...they're just doing their job as directed.

Sex indoctrination is just one of innumerable "exciting" and "innovative" self-indulgences of the schools. There is no bottom line test of what these boondoggles cost the children or the country.

Incidentally, conservatives who think that schools should be teaching "abstinence" miss the point completely. The schools have no expertise to be teaching sex in any form at all. We should be happy if they ever develop the competence to teach math and English, so that our children can hold their own in international tests given to children in other countries.

Yesteryear it was unnecessary...and today it would be unthinkable, but it would sure be refreshing to hear a no-nonsense school principal kickoff the new school year with an orientation like this:

To the students and faculty of our high school:

I am your new principal, and honored to be so. There is no greater calling than to teach young people.

I would like to apprise you of some important changes coming to our school. I am making these changes because I am convinced that most of the ideas that have dominated public education in America have worked against you, against your teachers and against our country.

First, this school will no longer honor race or ethnicity. I could not care less if your racial makeup is black, brown, red, yellow or white. I could not care less if your origins are African, Latin American, Asian or European, or if your ancestors arrived here on the Mayflower or on slave ships.

The only identity I care about, the only one this school will recognize, is your individual identity...your character, your scholarship, your humanity. And the only national identity this school will care about is American. This is an American public school, and American public schools were created to make better Americans.

If you wish to affirm an ethnic, racial or religious identity through school, you will have to go elsewhere. We will end all ethnicity, race...and non-American nationality-based celebrations. They undermine the motto of America, one of its three central values...e pluribus Unum, "from many, one." And this school will be guided by America's values.

This includes all after-school clubs. I will not authorize clubs that divide students based on any identities. This includes race, language, religion, sexual orientation or whatever else may become in vogue in a society divided by political correctness.

Your clubs will be based on interests and passions, not blood, ethnic, racial or other physically defined ties. Those clubs just cultivate narcissism...an unhealthy pre-occupation with the self, while the purpose of education is to get you to think beyond yourself. So we will have clubs that transport you to the wonders and glories of art, music, astronomy, languages you do not already speak, carpentry and more. If the only extracurricular activities you can imagine being interesting in are those based on ethnic, racial or sexual identity, that means that little outside of yourself really interests you.

Second, I am uninterested in whether English is your native language. My only interest in terms of language is that you leave this school speaking and writing English as fluently as possible. The English language has united America's citizens for over 200 years, and it will unite us at this school.

It is one of the indispensable reasons this country of immigrants has always come to be one country. And if you leave this school without excellent English language skills, I would be remiss in my duty to ensure that you will be prepared to successfully compete in the American job market. We will learn other languages here...it is deplorable that most Americans only speak English, but if you want classes taught in your native language rather than in English, this is not your school.

Third, because I regard learning as a sacred endeavor, everything in this school will reflect learning's elevated status. This means, among other things, that you and your teachers will dress accordingly. Many people in our society dress more formally for Hollywood events than for church or school. These people have their priorities backward. Therefore, there will be a formal dress code at this school.

Fourth, no obscene language will be tolerated anywhere on this school's property...whether in class, in the hallways or at athletic events. If you can't speak without using the f-word, you can't speak. By obscene language I mean the words banned by the Federal Communications Commission, plus epithets such as "Nigger," even when used by one black student to address another black, or "bitch," even when addressed by a girl to a girlfriend. It is my intent that by the time you leave this school, you will be among the few your age to instinctively distinguish between the elevated and the degraded, the holy and the obscene.

Fifth, we will end all self-esteem programs. In this school, self-esteem will be attained in only one way...the way people have always attained it, until decided otherwise a generation ago, by earning it. One immediate consequence is that there will only be one valedictorian, not eight.

Sixth, and last, I am reorienting the school toward academics and away from politics and propaganda. No more time will devoted to scaring you about smoking and caffeine, or terrifying you about sexual harassment or global warming. No more semesters will be devoted to condom wearing and teaching you to regard sexual relations as only or primarily a health issue.

There will be no more attempts to convince you that you are a victim because you are not white, or not male, or not heterosexual or not Christian. We will have failed if any one of you graduates this school and does not consider him or herself inordinately lucky...to be alive and to be an American.

Now, please stand and join me in the Pledge of Allegiance to the flag of our country. As many of you do not know the words, your teachers will hand them out to you.

But just so you know...throughout his presidency, Obama has decidedly and consistently not acted as a Progressive, though his rhetoric has consistently trended that way. For example, he has appointed economic advisors who were intimately involved in the events leading up to the current economic meltdown; he has failed to follow up on investigations of criminal misconduct of the Bush administration, in effect creating two tiers of justice...one for the powerful, and one for everyone else; his Department of Justice has offered up an extra-constitutional and specious theory of "sovereign immunity" to defend the flagrantly illegal wiretapping of Americans; and he has missed the opportunity of a generation to push for genuine reforms of corrupt banking and financial institutions, instead taking actions that benefit many of those most responsible for the corruption. His efforts to end wars that demand immediate cessation have been weak at best. In short, viewed collectively, his policy positions are decidedly to the right of Republican president Dwight Eisenhower. Those who have claimed that Obama is a "socialist" can have no idea whatsoever what that term means, and have failed completely to grasp the ideology actually reflected in his actions as President...or else he has intentionally promulgated grossly misleading characterizations.

Socialism is a philosophy of failure, the creed of ignorance, and the gospel of envy; its only inherent virtue is the equal sharing of misery.

Winston Churchill

CHAPTER 5

If he was around today, I would like to ask Mr. John Dewey, "So how's that progressive education system of yours working out for "us" today?

I find it interesting that the liberal/progressive community often view our Constitution (written by the best minds ever assembled) as an outdated relic from our distance past that falls far short of addressing our contemporary world today. But on the other hand, Dewey's progressive education curriculum (conceived by one man, over a 100 years ago) has endured and even grown in its acceptance within the liberal/progressive population. But that matters not, for unlike the Constitution, the progressive education system ducktails perfectly with our ever-expanding liberal/socialist world.

I also find it interesting that one of the major selling points for Dewey's new progressive education system was that it would produce a more engaged citizenry that would be better prepared to participate in not only their social interactions, but political and economic decisions that will ultimately affect everyone...America and the world at large.

It would now appear, with hindsight...that Dewey neglected to factor in the texting phenomenon that has engulfed our current citizenry. Younger folks today (generally speaking) are even more detached, distant and unengaged from the realities of life than they have ever been. But there's more to the bigger picture than just blaming the education system; I would also place plenty of culpability back with the parents who allowed and accepted this situation. Additionally, the traditional family unit has been in decline and taking with it, the family support groups that used to emphasize and encourage discipline, responsibility, accountability and above all... an appreciation of the "exceptionalism" of our country... America.

Congratulations, graduates...and condolences:

For those who matriculated at institutions of higher learning, you're likely to discover the job market isn't panting with anticipation to add you to its ranks. Now that you're out of college, you may just be added to the rolls of the over trained and under appreciated unemployed. It's not all your fault, but a good bit of it is.

For those who just escaped high school in caps and gowns, it's not too late to avoid four, five or six extremely expensive college years likely to lead you to a similar outcome. Those years, incidentally, can't be recaptured. You'll appreciate that last observation more as you age.

Excuse this writer for being the curmudgeon on the happy occasion of your graduation, but if I don't tell you, who will? Not only is a college education not necessarily all it's cracked up to be, it's not as necessary as you've been led to believe. Before I start receiving hate mail, allow me to stipulate some things.

A liberal arts education is eternally valuable, if not

necessarily highly valued today. A broad education in history, literature, science, math and language can benefit everyone. It makes well-rounded, cultured, sensitive and savvy citizens. We're in short supply of those. A liberal arts education can illustrate how to think critically, how to learn and how to understand how the world works.

A classic liberal arts education should prepare one for a meaningful life, equipping young people to answer life's important questions. Who am I? Why am I here? Where did I come from? Where am I going? What is the purpose of life? From there, it's much easier to determine how to behave and what to seek.

But such a liberal arts education could be administered largely in grades kindergarten through 12. But alas, those grades for decades have been given over in large-part to obsessions with political correctness, multiculturalism and teaching skills like slipping a condom over a banana, all "educational instructions" mankind managed to do without for centuries, and still grow into competent adulthood.

On Tuesday (7-5-2011), lawmakers in California sent the governor a bill to require public schools to include the contributions of gays and lesbians and other groups in social studies classes.

"This bill will require California schools to present a more accurate and nuanced view of American history," said Assembly Speaker John Perez, D-Los Angeles.

Assemblyman Tim Donnelly, R-Twin Peaks, said the bill was being used to promote a "homosexual agenda" in public schools.

Teaching is already required about women, African

Americans, Mexican Americans, Asian Americans, European Americans, American Indians, labor and entrepreneurs.

My question is, "Whatever happened to merit?" As a longtime California resident, I am so tired of our State Legislature's incessant placating of exclusive groups for political gain.

Enough is enough. Our children should be taught the contributions of famous Americans based on that person's contribution, not on an agenda of "Black history," "Jewish history," "women's history" or "gay history."

If that person's race, religion, gender or sexual identity was a factor in their contribution to history, then by all means make note of it. But to call a group out solely for the purpose of calling it out diminishes the individual contributors and belittles members of those groups who have worked so hard to realize the California dream based on merit alone.

But not every criticism here is a blanket condemnation. There are many exceptions. Still, there is enough veracity in what follows that you should pause to rethink whether college is necessary.

Career path to nowhere:

College has morphed from a place to search for truth to a factory seeking to manufacture candidates for lucrative employment. Not only are countless young people now being "educated" minus the liberal arts foundation, they are also being misled to believe they are preparing for well-paying careers.

In 1992, says the U.S. Bureau of Labor Statistics, 119,000 college degree-holders were waiters and waitresses, probably something of a disappointment for them. By 2008, that number was 318,000. One out of five new waiter and waitress jobs were filled by college grads.

It's commonly understood that today's college degree is roughly equivalent to yesterday's high school diploma. Richard Vedder's research discovered that 60 percent of the increase in college graduates from 1992-to-2008 worked in what the government considers relatively low-skilled jobs, where co-workers have high school diplomas or less.

It's true that engineering majors have the highest median annual earnings, $85,000 to $105,000...but someone has to be at the top, right? Counseling and psychology majors' median annual salary is $29,000, says Georgetown University's Center on Education and the Workforce. Majors in *community organizations*, whatever those are, average $38,000. I guess it's possible to go on to become *president* from such beginnings, but the odds seem long.

Then there's the million-dollar myth. It's frequently asserted that college graduation leads to a $1 million boost in lifetime earnings compared with a high-school education. Not by a long shot. American Enterprise Institute found the lifetime earnings gap to be much less, $150,000 to $500,000, after accounting for years of foregone wages while students are out of the workplace and for the costs of paying for college. Spread over four decades, that's much less inspiring.

Sticker shock:

How shall we put this next point delicately? College is a racket. College costs are increasing faster than inflation, faster than home prices, and they are spurred on by third-party payers, through grants and loans, largely from the government, which means from taxpayers. In 2008-09, federal, state and institutional student aid totaled $168 billion; in 1998-99 it was $89 billion. As we see with Medicare, Medicaid and employer-paid health insurance, when third parties foot the bill, prices rise, and demand increases. Thanks to the woeful, if well-intentioned, government dispensing of other peoples' money, the typical college graduate steps off campus and into huge debt. In 2008, the average graduating senior with student loans owed $23,200, 24 percent more than the average four years earlier.

And, thanks to that huge debt, grads have about a one-in-eight chance of being deadbeats. About 467,000 students, 13.8 percent of student loan borrowers, defaulted in 2008 within three years of beginning repayment.

What's all this spending, borrowing and loan reneging buying?

"Too many of the people coming out of our most prestigious academic institutions graduate with neither the skills to be economically productive nor the intellectual development to make them discerning citizens and voters," economist Thomas Sowell recently wrote. Sowell explained one reason is that so many young people crowding college classrooms are taking courses "weighted toward the soft end of the spectrum." He's not talking about math and science.

Only about 65 percent of California State University students even bothered to attend class after the third week in the 20-year teaching experience of Victor Davis Hanson.

"Most faculty members at CSU would probably admit privately that a large minority of their students simply do not do the work or attend class regularly," Hanson recently wrote in the National Review's...The Corner blog. "The point is not to bash the students or the faculty, but to ask the university to reexamine the way it does business."

Columnist Mona Charen also pointed out recently...that 50 leading colleges that required courses in Western Civilization in 1964, no longer do. The same is true for American history, she noted.

Possible remedies:

What might universities do differently? For starters, they might turn away the unprepared and ill equipped. More than 50 percent of incoming CSU freshmen must take remedial classes in the university before they can take normal courses.

CSU is infuriating, but it isn't unique. Nationwide, education mills collecting tens of thousands of dollars per head while shoving raw, unqualified students through their sausage-making machinery, irrespective of whether they belong.

This rant won't repair the damage, but it should be a caution. For college grads, this advice comes too late. But for high school graduates, ask yourselves if your earliest adult years are best spent back-filling the gaps of your deficient high school education at a cost of $20,000 to $40,000 a year? Are five-figure college loan debts the best way to embark on adult life? Do you really want to renege on those loans?

Best advice? First, determine what you want. Then, once you know, don't be deterred. But until you know, a broad sampling through a true liberal arts education can be invaluable for finding out.

The world is increasingly technical, but technical stuff isn't necessarily college stuff. Trade schools offer reasonable alternatives. Take a quick inventory: How many people making a living on the Internet were trained in a college to do what they do?

Frankly, I believe we would be better off if universities returned to a classic, liberal arts mission and left specializations such as engineering, medicine and computer science to, well, specialized institutions.

More bad news:

> Only 12 percent of high school seniors are "proficient" in history. As philosopher George Santayana observed, "Those who cannot remember the past are condemned to repeat it."

> Thanks to texting, we are raising a generation that doesn't speak English properly and spells phonetically.

> We have become a country without moral absolutes; philosophers, historians and anthropologists pretty much agree that when a society abandons any semblance of moral absolutism...supplanted by moral relativism, that culture is decaying.

Unless the electorate speaks up, the foregoing says a lot about the decline of the American Republic.

CHAPTER 6

A universal education for every child in this country was a beautiful dream, but it hasn't succeeded.

Public education throughout this country is failing or has already failed in too many school districts. "A Nation at Risk: The Imperative for Educational Reform," was released in April 1983. It is just as true today, if not more so. A friend of mine taught at the same school and same grade for 36 years. He recently told me that the students he had back in the beginning of his tenure far outperformed the students he had in his closing years.

There is no simple or single cause for public education's ongoing collapse. Parents can blame schools, teachers can blame parents, and politicians can blame taxpayers for not throwing more money at the problem. The first two viewpoints may have some merit, but the problem with public education is definitely not enough money. Instead, politicians, by vastly expanding the educational bureaucracy, are stifling public schools. Big Education, like big anything else, is less efficient and more expensive. Yet, this is the system our politicians have created.

In Anna Sewell's literary classic, "Black Beauty," there

is a poignant scene where a taxicab horse, Ginger, is being whipped by the driver for not being able to pull an overloaded cab fast enough. As an allegory, if you consider the taxi driver the government's educational policy makers, the passengers as the students in schools, the overloaded cab as the things required of teachers, and the taxi horse as the teachers, you can come pretty close to what is wrong with the public education.

Are there bad teachers? Of course there are. Are there ineffective administrators? Absolutely. Is part of the problem uninvolved parents and unmotivated students? Yes.

However, none of these factors has impacted the success of public education as much as the big government's edicts to local school districts. Decisions are being made and policies enforced by people far removed from the classroom. Some of these decision makers, like Secretary of Education Arne Duncan, have never been teachers. Some are ivory-tower educators whose teaching experience is mostly theoretical. Others may have been teachers for a while, but have forgotten what life is like in the educational trenches.

One of the more interesting TV reality shows is "Undercover Boss." The show takes a high-level executive of a big business and places him or her in an entry-level job at his or her own company. In most episodes, the bosses have their eyes opened, big time.

If some of the educational bureaucrats, at all levels, had to implement the policies they decree, schools would operate much more realistically. Say, for instance, that the educational theorists who, concerned for children's self-esteem, decided that retention after first grade was a bad idea, had to deal with children working years behind grade level in an upper-grade class. Children working three or four years below grade level know they aren't keeping up, so their self-esteem still suffers. This often leads to off-task behavior that detracts from the learning process for themselves and others. Actual classroom experience might help change some top-down driven ideas about dealing with such things as discipline problems and many other obstacles teachers face as well.

That is the problem with the government's influence and control of public schools. People who don't teach mandate what to teach and how to teach it. Thus, teachers, like the taxicab horse Ginger, are told to pull ever-heavier loads. One consequence, of course, is that the students in the cab aren't getting where they need to go. I cannot count how many times my friend told me about new programs he was expected to implement that just didn't work, wasted his time, wasted the students' time, and cost money, and didn't help students anyway. If a student is identified "At Risk" in second grade and, after six years of costly interventions, is still not successful, something isn't working.

Public education decision makers have been aware for a long time that the system hasn't been working. Those who make the policies have come up with dozens of "magic bullets" over the years, programs or new teaching methods they thought would fix the problems of public education, but they haven't.

I would add that this progressive system of government-facilitated education is also the driver behind the systematic rewriting of history:

In the conclusion of "Adventures of Huckleberry Finn," the protagonist and narrator notes, "There ain't nothing more to write about, and I am rotten glad of it, because if I'd a knowed what a trouble it was to make a book...I wouldn't a tackled it, and ain't a going to no more. The End. Yours Truly, Huck Finn."

Creating mixed reviews and fueling controversy since it was first published in 1885, Mark Twain's quintessential novel remains a lasting classic to this day, on a par with renowned novels such as "The Grapes of Wrath" and "The Catcher in the Rye."

Unfortunately, it has also been banned periodically because of its coarse language, racial stereotypes and racial slurs. Most recently, some school districts began using a newly available alternative version that is rewritten without offensive language. But is the banning of these classics or using alternative versions actually protecting children? And are the concerns of those who support banning such classics legitimate?

I read Adventures of Huckleberry Finn, as a teenager growing up in Arkansas, and as an adult I watched the PBS documentary Born to Trouble: Adventures of Huck Finn, which gave meaningful insight into critical issues such as censorship and race. The documentary led me to the conclusion that the novel is far from being racist.

If we understand the political and social background in which Adventures of Huckleberry Finn was written, we realize that Twain's use of racial slurs and stereotypes are used to accurately portray the setting and mood of the antebellum South, and not to demean blacks. It is ironic how the novel is frequently criticized for its racism even though Mark Twain intended for the book to condemn the injustice of slavery. Critics have often cited Huck's moral awakening to the injustices of slavery as one of the most profound literary statements against racial prejudice.

Objections typically focus on the negative characterization of the black slave Jim and Twain's repeated use of the "n-word." Although Twain may have used a negative stereotype to create his character, Jim's humanity behind his minstrel façade is consistently shown. As Huck's companion, Jim shows both compassion and intelligence and acts as a fatherly figure to the young boy. Both noble and loyal, Jim is one of the few adults in the novel that sets an honorable example for Huck to follow.

Versions of Huck Finn have been produced replacing the n-word with the word "slave." However, by removing the racial slurs, which are used ironically, we are undermining Mark Twain's message. Such slurs should offend us because that is the exact effect Twain intended. Slurs are used to accurately portray the setting of the story and not as a way to approve of their use during that time period. By pretending that Twain never used slurs in Huck Finn and publishing an alternative version, we diminish the quality of a great American novel and do students a great disservice by distorting the historical reality of racial discrimination.

The solution to the problem of presenting the literary value of this novel to a classroom of adolescents without offending anyone is not to ban it, as many schools across the nation have done. Simply offering those who object a different novel of the same level effectively solves the problem. By no means should those students who refuse to read Huck Finn deprive an entire school of the opportunity to enjoy such a classic.

Is banning or censoring books beneficial for young people or, more importantly, ethical? The answer is clearly no. By banning major works, we deprive students of the opportunity to broaden their literary horizons and reduce a students' ability to think critically. By reading potentially troubling or mature content, students are exposed to the reality of society and learn to draw their own conclusions on controversial issues.

One should be offered an alternate text of the same level to read if he or she feels uncomfortable for whatever reason. I also think it is important and helpful for teachers to have discussed the issue of race in America before students actually read the novel. And reading the book should encourage students to respect each other and discourage them from making racially offensive comments.

By introducing controversial themes through various texts, schools encourage students to discuss sensitive topics, hear the viewpoints of their peers and develop maturity. The benefits that come with reading thought-provoking classics far outweigh any detriment.

As Mark Twain himself said, "When people let Huck Finn alone he goes peacefully along, damaging a few children here and there and yonder, but...it is no great matter. By and by, let us hope, people that really have the best interests of the rising generations at heart, will become wise and not stir Huck up."

But there are even bigger internal problems festering and fed by personal and corporate greed. It was recently reported that the Atlanta Public Schools system has spent the last decade systemically cheating on its tests. Not the students, but some 44 of the 56 school districts, superintendents, the union, 38 principals, and at least 178 teachers, whoops...pardon me, "educators." Teachers apparently held "changing parties" at their homes where they sat around with extra supplies of erasers correcting their students' test answers in order to improve their overall scores and qualify for "No Child Left Behind" federal funding that could be sluiced into maintaining their lavish remuneration. Let's face it; it's easier than teaching, right?

The Atlanta Public Schools' Human Resources honcho, Millicent Few, had an earlier report, warning her about suspected test tampering, illegally destroyed. So the Atlanta Public Schools system not only got the federal

THE COMPROMISING OF AMERICA

gravy but was also held up to the nation at large as a heartwarming, inspirational example of how large urban school districts can reform themselves and improve educational opportunities for their children.

And its fake test scores got its leader, Beverly Hall, garlanded with the National Superintendent of the Year Award, the Administrator of the Year Award, the Distinguished Public Service Award, the Keystone Award for Leadership in Education, the Concerned Black Clergy Education Award, the American Association of School Administrators Effie H. Jones Humanitarian Award and a zillion other phony-baloney baubles with which the American education-fraud cartel scratches its own back.

In reality, Beverly Hall's Atlanta Public Schools system was in the child-abuse business. It violated the education of its students to improve its employees' cozy sinecures.

The whole rotten stinking school system is systemically corrupt from the superintendent down. But what are the chances of the Atlanta Public Schools being closed down? How many of those fraudulent non-teachers will waft on within the system until their lucrative retirements?

So...how about those moral absolutes...or lack of?

Just another example of the self-serving corruption that has infested ever layer of our pyramid of government sponsored public servants. The level of government matters not, preservation is always an under laying motivation...protecting one's butt. Yes, corruption is rampant in the public sector also...but my taxes aren't "directly" paying their salaries.

These policy makers might better ask why so many private schools outperform traditional public schools, and do so at a lower cost. If they did, they would realize that private schools have greater local control of their curriculum, and teachers can spend more time working with students. The students are more motivated, not only because the students' parents are paying directly out of their own pockets for their children's education, but have also instilled the idea in their children that education is important. Discipline problems do not distract from the learning process because private schools, unlike public schools, have the luxury of removing problem students.

The dream of a universal education was, and is, a noble one, but our public schools are not able to implement it under the present conditions.

Schools are just one of many government institutions that take on tasks for which they have no expertise or even competence. Congress is the most egregious example. In the course of any given year, Congress votes on taxes, medical care, military spending, foreign aid, agriculture, labor, international trade, airlines, housing, insurance, courts, natural resources, and much more.

There are professionals who have spent their entire adult lives specializing in just one of these fields. The idea that Congress can be competent in all these areas simultaneously is staggering. Yet, far from pulling back, as banks or other private enterprises must, if they don't want to be ruined financially by operating beyond the range of their competence...Congress is constantly expanding further into more fields.

Having spent years ruining the housing markets with their interference, leading to a housing meltdown that has taken the whole economy down with it, politicians have now moved on into micro-managing automobile companies and medical care.

They are not going to stop unless they get stopped. And that is not going to happen until the voters recognize the fact that political rhetoric is no substitute for competence.

I find it interesting that some of the Progressives' core values are wrapped around phrases like justice for all, the people, civil liberties and opposition to large corporations. I would suggest that our government has become the largest conglomerate of all and that it's currently walking all over "we the peoples."

I've spent so much time badmouthing our educational machinery because education is the foundation for a prosperous, stable and free country. Look around and think about it, what are some of the commonalities connecting the world's Third World countries? I would say, "Little to no formal education, poverty and widespread corruption within their governments."

CHAPTER 7

Many of our nation's problems are a direct result of our being immune, hostile or indifferent to several moral questions: If a person benefits from a hamburger, a suit of clothing, an apartment or an education, who should be forced to pay for it? I believe the question has only one moral answer, namely the person who benefited from the items or services should be forced to pay for those things; that's if we wish to distinguish ourselves from common thieves who only care about enjoying the fruits of our caring and bountiful country...and who pays is irrelevant.

Those who view government entitlement programs as sacrosanct, and regard those who want to cut them back as calloused or cruel, picture a world very different from the world of reality.

To listen to some of the defenders of entitlement programs, which are at the heart of our present financial crisis, you might think that anything the government fails to provide is something that people will be deprived of.

In other words, if you cut spending on school lunches, children will go hungry. If you fail to subsidize housing, people will be homeless. If you fail to subsidize prescription drugs, old people will have to eat dog food in order to be able to afford their meds.

This is the vision promoted by many politicians and much of the media. But, in the world of reality, it is not even true for most people who are living below the official poverty line.

Most Americans living below the official poverty line own a car or truck...and government entitlement programs seldom provide cars and trucks. Most people living below the official poverty line also have air conditioning, color television and a microwave oven...and these too are not usually handed out by government entitlement programs.

Cell phones and other electronic devices are by no means unheard of in low-income neighborhoods, where children would supposedly go hungry if there were no school lunch programs. In reality, low-income people are overweight even more often than other Americans.

As for housing and homelessness, housing prices are higher and homelessness a bigger problem in places where there has been massive government intervention, such as liberal bastions like New York City and San Francisco. As for the elderly, 80 percent are homeowners whose monthly housing costs are less than $400, including property taxes, utilities, and maintenance.

The desperately poor elderly conjured up in political and media rhetoric is, in the world of reality...the wealthiest segment of the American population. The average wealth of older households is nearly three times the wealth of households headed by people in the 35-to-44-year-old bracket, and more than 15 times the wealth of households headed by someone under 35 years of age.

If the wealthiest segment of the population cannot pay all their medical bills, and who can; the country as a whole is not any richer because the government pays those medical bills...with money that it takes from us.

What about the truly poor, in whatever age brackets? First of all, even in low-income and high-crime neighborhoods, people are not stealing bread to feed their children. The fraction of the people in such neighborhoods who commit most of the crimes are far more likely to steal luxury products that they can either use or sell to get money to support their parasitic lifestyle.

As for the rest of the poor, Professor Walter Williams of George Mason University long ago showed that you could give the poor enough money to lift them all above the official poverty line for a fraction of what it costs to support a massive welfare state bureaucracy.

We don't need to send the country into bankruptcy, in the name of the poor, by spending trillions of dollars on people who are not poor, and who could take care of themselves. The poor have been used as human shields behind which the expanding welfare state can advance.

The goal is not to keep the poor from starving but to create dependency, because dependency translates into votes for politicians who play Santa Claus.

We have all heard the old saying about how giving a man a fish feeds him for a day, while teaching him to fish feeds him for a lifetime. Independence makes for a healthier society, but dependency is what gets votes for politicians.

For politicians, giving a man a fish every day of his life is the way to keep getting his vote. "Entitlement" is just a fancy word for dependency. As for the scary stories politicians tell, in order to keep the entitlement programs going, as long as we keep buying it, they will keep selling it.

One of the painfully revealing episodes in Barack Obama's book "Dreams From My Father" describes his early experience listening to a sermon by the Reverend Jeremiah Wright. Among the things said in that sermon was that "white folks' greed runs a world in need." Obama was literally moved to tears by that sermon.

This sermon may have been like a revelation to Barack Obama, but its explanation of economic and other differences between the races was among the oldest, and most factually discredited explanations of such disparity among all sorts of peoples in all sorts of places. Yet it is an explanation that has long been politically seductive in countries around the world.

What could be more emotionally satisfying than seeing others who have done better in the world as the villains responsible for your not having done as well? It is the ideal political explanation, from the standpoint of mass appeal, whether or not it makes any sense otherwise.

That has been the politically preferred explanation for economic differences between the Malay majority and the more prosperous Chinese minority in Malaysia, or between the Gentile majority and the Jewish minority in various countries in Europe, between the two World Wars.

At various other times and places, it has been the preferred explanation for the economic differences between the Sinhalese and the Tamil minority in Sri Lanka, the Africans and the Lebanese in Sierra Leone, the Czechs and the Germans in Bohemia and numerous other groups in countries around the world.

The idea that the rich have gotten rich by making the poor, poor...has been an ideological theme that has played well in Third World countries, to explain why they lag so far behind the West.

None of this was original with Jeremiah Wright. All he added was his own colorful gutter style of expressing it, which so captivated the man who is now President of the United States.

There is obviously something there with very deep emotional appeal. Moreover, because nothing is easier to find than sins among human beings, there will never be a lack of evil deeds to make that explanation seem plausible.

Because the Western culture has been ascendant in the world in recent centuries, the image of rich white people and poor non-white people has made a deep impression, whether in theories of racial superiority...which was big among "progressives" in the early 20th century, or in theories of exploitation among "progressives" later on... more politically correct.

Coincidentally, a few days ago I stumbled upon a research article that investigated the time our young people spend engaged in media, social networking and various other Internet and communication apps. I was not surprised to find that children/young people who spend the most time in those venues do worse in school. It went on to say that Black and Hispanic kids (on average) consume 4-1/2 hours more media-hours per day than White kids. If you hadn't heard about this, I'm not surprised...it's just that nobody has found a way to connect it to racism.

In a wider view of history, however, it becomes clear that, for centuries before the European ascendancy, Europe lagged far behind China in many achievements. Since neither of them changed much genetically between those times and the later rise of Europe, it is hard to reconcile this role reversal with racial theories.

More importantly, the Chinese were not to blame for Europe's problems, which would not be solved until the Europeans themselves finally got their own act together, instead of blaming others. If they had listened to people like Jeremiah Wright, Europe might still be in the Dark Ages.

It is hard to reconcile "exploitation" theories with the facts. While there have been conquered peoples made poorer by their conquerors, especially by Spanish conquerors in the Western Hemisphere, but generally...most poor countries were poor for reasons that existed before the conquerors arrived. Some Third World countries are poorer today than they were when they were ruled by Western countries, generations ago.

False theories are not just an intellectual problem to be discussed around a seminar table in some ivy-covered building. When millions of people believe those theories, including people in high places, with the fate of nations in their hands, that is a serious and potentially disastrous fact of life.

Despite a carefully choreographed image of affability and cool, Barack Obama's decisions and appointments as President betray an alienation from the values and the people of this country that are too disturbing to be answered by showing his birth certificate.

Too many of his appointees exhibit a similar alienation, including Attorney General Eric Holder, under whom the Department of Justice could more accurately be described as the Department of Payback.

An add to the payback conjecture: The late South African economist William Hutt, in his 1964 book, "The Economics of the Colour Bar," said that one of the supreme tragedies of the human condition is that those who have been the victims of injustices and oppression "can often be observed to be inflicting not dissimilar injustices upon other races." Born in 1936, I have lived through some of our openly racist history, which has included racist insults, beatings and lynching. Today, all that has changed, blacks commit most racist assaults. What's worse is there are blacks, still alive today, who lived through those times of lynching, Jim Crow laws and open racism who remain silent in the face of our new, "unacknowledged racism."

Our fight today is about whether we are, most fundamentally, a welfare state in which government runs the show, or whether this is a free country, in which free, private citizens run the show.

"I think we have more machinery of government than is necessary and too many parasites living on the labor of the industrious."

Thomas Jefferson

CHAPTER 8

I find it disturbing that the world's exploding population isn't a top priority of every government in the world. Instead of concentrating on this problem, which is destroying the planet, most are more interested in addressing the symptoms generated by our overpopulation.

We are more concerned about high-energy costs, not enough food to feed the world's ever-expanding population and the greenhouse effect, which is changing our climate (they say). These are just a few of the problems caused by too many people on a small planet.

The U.S. government is actually encouraging a much larger population for our country. Traditionally, we have allowed a quarter million immigrants into our country annually, which is more than any other country permits, but in recent years we have been accepting more than a million a year, even during this recession.

The Census Bureau estimates, at the current rate of growth, the United States will reach a population of 1,182,000,000 by the turn of the next century. This will be almost totally due to immigration and government shortsightedness.

We are a nation of immigrants, but we must face the fact that too many people will destroy our environment and our way of life.

Many of you are already aware of some the staggering effects of mass immigration on health care and poverty. For instance:

> 71 percent of the increase in America's uninsured, since 1989, is the result of immigrants and their children.

> 57 percent of immigrant households (both legal and illegal) with children use at least one welfare program.

The election last year (2010) gave us what might have been our last chance to get it right, especially here in California, after getting it wrong so often in the past. We needed to vote out the social progressives whose policies are so damaging to our society. They are dangerous to our way of life. But, we returned too many incumbents back to their offices, where they can enact still more destructive programs that will change the United States into a copy of a Western Europe-type social democracy.

With the recent riots in France and Greece, Germany's Chancellor Angela Merkel admitted that German multiculturalism had "utterly failed," and with the threatened debt defaults in country after country, the peril to our country should be obvious. Germany's failure in multiculturalism isn't an anomaly, it's the norm throughout Europe...Chancellor Merkel just had the fortitude to say it out loud, in spite of the political incorrectness of her declaration. Americans are just beginning to feel the tension associated with our non-assimilating, multiculturalism country. But rest assured, it's coming and we're barely seeing the tip of the iceberg. This administration is promoting and sponsoring the invasion...and the inevitable disruption of the American way of life, as we've always known it.

Do we really want a cradle-to-grave Nanny State telling us how to live our lives? President Gerald Ford said it best: "A government big enough to give you everything you want is a government big enough to take from you everything you have."

One more thing to remember when voting is that the social progressive leadership is not incompetent, but calculating. Take the social progressive stance toward manmade climate change as an example. Notice that the term is now "climate change" and not global warming. That is a calculated change. While I absolutely believe in global climate change, after all, there have been at least five major ice ages in the history of the Earth, the most recent ending about 10,000 years ago when the total human population was probably around 1 million individuals. There is no way a million people could have burned enough campfires to affect the carbon output worldwide. That doesn't matter to the rank-and-file progressives who believe whatever their leaders tell them. These liberals are what Lenin termed "useful idiots." Unfortunately, for the heads of the social progressives, there aren't enough useful idiots to elect the social progressive leadership by themselves.

Therefore, in a calculated move to ensure their power, the leaders of the social progressives have been deliberately creating an underclass in America. A large group dependent on the government for their well-being, thereby garnering the additional votes necessary to continue in power. Something like 47 percent of the American electorate now receives some kind of government largess. Food stamp recipients now number close to 42 million, up by almost 10 million since President Barack Obama's election. Millions more get SSI, even if they didn't contribute to Social Security in the first place.

In addition, of course there are the federal tax refunds for millions of "taxpayers" who didn't pay federal taxes. Public sector employees not only average more in salary than their private sector equivalents, the pensions for public employees are yet another entitlement we can't afford. The list of abuses of the system is never-ending. Now, while we are told that this is compassion, it really isn't. It's just a ploy by progressives to increase their voter base.

Don't get me wrong; politicians have been doing this for a long, long time, just never to this scale. As irritating as hundreds of millions of taxpayer dollars earmarked for political pork projects are, that pales in comparison with the over $13.5 trillion public debt. President Obama has increased the national debt by 3 trillion dollars since his election.

Those social progressives in power must know that our current spending is unsustainable. Then why the spending, you ask? I believe it is to meet one of their dearest goals...wealth redistribution. As candidate Obama told "Joe the plumber," he wants to "spread the wealth around." In order to pay for all the programs he wants passed, taxes will have to be raised.

Some of the proposed tax increases are downright scary:

> A transaction tax of 1 percent on all transactions at any financial institution, like your bank or credit union.

> A value-added tax, which in Europe, adds about 19 percent to the cost of everything.

> ➢ New taxes on carbon emissions, which of course, companies would pass along to their customers.

The president's financial team is discussing these taxes, and others, but of course, their report will not come out until after the 2012 election.

President Obama pledged to "fundamentally change" America. We need to take him at his word and stop him. Remember, his wife called America a country that is "just downright mean." If you believe that, you would want to change things.

Again, consider Western Europe as their model. It won't work, but because social progressives put their ideology ahead of common sense, we are headed for disaster. If the Democrats had lost both houses of Congress what do you think the odds would have been that the lame ducks would have bowed out gracefully to the will of the people? Even losing the House hasn't been a deterrent as Obama and his minions continue their senseless, spending marathon.

The typical lawmaker of today is a man devoid of principle...a mere counter in a grotesque and knavish games. If the right pressure should be applied to him he would cheerfully be in favor of polygamy, astrology or cannibalism.

H. L. Mencken

CHAPTER 9

We know Dick Lamm as the former Governor of Colorado. In that context his thoughts are particularly poignant. On September 1, 2006, there was an immigration overpopulation conference in Washington, DC, filled to capacity by many of America's finest minds and leaders. A brilliant college professor by the name of Victor Hansen Davis talked about his latest book, "Mexifornia," explaining how immigration...both legal and illegal was destroying the entire state of California. He said it would march across the country until it destroyed all vestiges of The American Dream.

Moments later, former Colorado Governor Richard D. Lamm stood up and gave a stunning speech on how to destroy America. The audience sat spellbound as he described eight methods for the destruction of the United States. He said, "If you believe that America is too smug, too self-satisfied, too rich, then let's destroy America. It is not that hard to do. No nation in history has survived the ravages of time. Arnold Toynbee observed that all great civilizations rise and fall and that 'an autopsy of history' would show that all great nations commit suicide."

"Here is how they do it," Lamm said:

First, to destroy America, turn America into a bilingual or multi-lingual and bicultural country. History shows that no nation can survive the tension, conflict, and antagonism of two or more competing languages and cultures. It is a blessing for an individual to be bilingual; however, it is a curse for a society to be bilingual. The historical scholar, Seymour Lipset, put it this way, "The histories of bilingual and bicultural societies that do not assimilate are histories of turmoil, tension, and tragedy." Canada, Belgium, Malaysia, and Lebanon all face crises of national existence in which minorities press for autonomy, if not independence. Pakistan and Cyprus have divided. Nigeria suppressed an ethnic rebellion. France faces difficulties with Basques, Bretons, Corsicans and Muslims. It was also a major problem for the USSR.

Lamm went on:

Second, to destroy America, invent "multiculturalism" and encourage immigrants to maintain their culture. Make it an article of belief that all cultures are equal, that there are no cultural differences. Make it an article of faith that the Black and Hispanic dropout rates are due solely to prejudice and discrimination by the majority. Every other explanation is out of bounds.

Third, we could make the United States a "Hispanic Quebec" without much effort. The key is to celebrate diversity rather than unity. As Benjamin Schwarz said in the Atlantic Monthly recently, "The apparent success of our own multi-ethnic and multicultural experiment might have been achieved not by tolerance but by hegemony. Without the dominance that once dictated ethnocentrism and what it meant to be an American, we are left with only tolerance and pluralism to hold us together."

Lamm said, "I would encourage all immigrants to keep their own language and culture. I would replace the melting pot metaphor with the salad bowl metaphor. It is important to ensure that we have various cultural subgroups living in America enforcing their differences rather than as Americans, emphasizing their similarities."

Fourth, I would make our fastest growing demographic group the least educated. I would add a second underclass, unassimilated, undereducated, and antagonistic to our population. I would have this second underclass have a 50 percent dropout rate from high school.

My fifth point for destroying America would be to get big foundations and business to give these efforts lots of money. I would invest in ethnic identity, and I would establish the cult of "Victimology." I would get all minorities to think that their lack of success was the fault of the majority. I would start a grievance industry blaming all minority failure on the majority population.

My sixth plan for America's downfall would include dual citizenship, promote divided loyalties and would celebrate diversity over unity. I would stress differences rather than similarities. Diverse people worldwide are mostly engaged in hating each other...that is when they are not killing each other. A diverse, peaceful, or stable society is against most historical precepts. People undervalue the unity it takes to keep a nation together.

Look at the ancient Greeks. The Greeks believed that they belonged to the same race; they possessed a common language and literature, and they worshipped the same gods. All Greece took part in the Olympic games. A common enemy, Persia, threatened their liberty. Yet all those bonds were not strong enough to overcome two factors: local patriotism and geographical conditions that nurtured political divisions. Greece fell.

Next to last, I would place certain subjects off limits. Make it taboo to talk about anything against the cult of "diversity." I would find a word similar to "heretic" in the 16th century that stopped discussion and paralyzed thinking. Words like "racist" or "xenophobe" to halt discussion and debate. Having made America a bilingual/bicultural country, having established multi-cultism, having the large foundations fund the doctrine of Victimology, I would next make it impossible to enforce our immigration laws. I would develop a mantra: that because immigration has been good for America, it must always be good. I would make every individual immigrant symmetric and ignore the cumulative impact of millions of them.

In the last minute of his speech, Governor Lamm wiped his brow. Profound silence followed. Finally he said, "Lastly, I would censor Victor Hanson Davis's book Mexifornia. His book is dangerous. It exposes the plan to destroy America. If you feel America deserves to be destroyed, then don't read that book."

There was no applause. A chilling fear quietly rose like an ominous cloud above every attendee at the conference. Every American in that room knew that everything Lamm enumerated was proceeding methodically, quietly, darkly, yet pervasively across the United States today.

Discussion is being suppressed. Over 100 languages are ripping the foundation of our educational system and national cohesiveness. Even barbaric cultures that practice female genital mutilation are growing as we celebrate "diversity." American jobs are vanishing into the Third World as corporations create a Third World in America. Take note of not only California, but also our other states. To date, ten to eleven million illegal aliens and growing fast.

Governor Lamm walked back to his seat. It dawned on everyone at the conference that our nation and the future of this great democracy are deeply in trouble and worsening fast. If we don't get this immigration monster stopped within three years, it will rage like a California wildfire and destroy everything in its path, especially The American Dream.

It is reminiscent of George Orwell's book "1984." In that story, three slogans are engraved in the Ministry of Truth building: "War is peace," "Freedom is slavery," and "Ignorance is strength."

CHAPTER 10

I n the Spring, 2002 issue of City Journal, Victor Hanson Davis wrote an essay about growing up in the central San Joaquin Valley and witnessing firsthand, especially over the last 20 years, the ill effects of illegal immigration. Controversy over his blunt assessment of the disaster of illegal immigration from Mexico led to an expanded memoir, "Mexifornia," published the following year by Encounter Press.

Mexifornia came out during the ultimately successful campaign to recall California governor Gray Davis in autumn 2003. A popular public gripe was that the embattled governor had appeased both employers and the more radical Hispanic politicians of the California legislature on illegal immigration. And indeed Davis had signed legislation allowing driver's licenses for illegal aliens that both houses of state government had passed. So it was no wonder that the book sometimes found its way into both the low and high forms of the political debate. On the Internet, a close facsimile of a California driver's license circulated, with a picture of a Mexican bandit (the gifted actor Alfonso Bedoya of The Treasure of the Sierra Madre), together with a demeaning height (5'- 4"), weight (too much), and sex (mucho) given. "Mexifornia" was emblazoned across the top where "California" usually is stamped on the license.

In such a polarized climate, heated debates and several radio interviews followed, often with the query, "Why did you have to write such a book?" The Left saw the book's arguments and its title as unduly harsh to newcomers from Mexico. Mexifornia was originally a term of approbation used by activists buoyed by California's changing demography. The Right saw the book as long-over-due attention to a scandal ignored by the mainstream Republican Party.

Fast-forward nearly five years, and the national climate has radically changed so much that deportation, which was once an unimaginable response to the problem of the 11 million here illegally, is now practicality, rather than morality, and has become the keener point of contention. The concerted effort by Chicano activists to drive popular parlance from the descriptive term "illegal alien" in favor of the politically correct, but imprecise and often misleading "undocumented worker" has largely failed. Similar efforts to demonize opponents of open borders as "anti-immigrant" or "nativist" have had only a marginal effect in stifling debate, as has the deliberate effort to blur illegal and legal immigration. The old utopian talk of a new borderless zone of dual cultures, spreading on both sides of a disappearing boundary, has given way to a reexamination of NAFTA and its facilitation of greater cross-border flows of goods, services...and illegal aliens and drugs.

So why has the controversy over illegal immigration moved so markedly to the right?

We must always return to the question of numbers. While it is true that no one knows exactly how many are here illegally from Mexico and Latin America, both sides in the debate often accept, as reasonable, estimates of 11 to 12 million illegals...with an additional 500,000 to 1 million arriving per year. Given porous borders, such guesses about the number of illegal aliens in the United States are outdated almost as soon as they are published. It is plausible, then, that there may be an additional 3 to 4 million illegal aliens here who were not here when the City Journal "Mexifornia" piece appeared.

The result of such staggering numbers is that aliens now don't just cluster in the American Southwest but frequently appear at Home Depot parking lots in the Midwest, emergency rooms in New England, and construction sites in the Carolinas, making illegal immigration an American, rather than a mere Californian or Arizonan, concern.

Indeed, we forget how numbers are at the crux of the entire debate over illegal immigration. In the 1970s, perhaps a few million illegals resided in the United States, and their unassimilated presence went largely unnoticed. Most Americans felt that the formidable powers of integration and popular culture would continue to incorporate any distinctive ethnic enclave, as they had so successfully done with the past generations that arrived en masse from Europe, Asia, and Latin America. But when more than 10 million fled Mexico in little over a decade...the great majority poor, without English, job skills, a high school education, or legality, entire apartheid communities in the American Southwest began springing up.

During the heyday of multiculturalism and political correctness in the 1980s, our response...as the hosts, to this novel challenge was not to insist upon the traditional assimilation of the newcomers but rather to accommodate the illegal alien with official Spanish-language documents, bilingual education, and ethnic boosterism in our media, politics, and education. These responses only encouraged more illegals to come, on the guarantee that their material life could be better and yet their culture unchanged in the United States. We now see the results. Los Angeles is today the second-largest Mexican city in the world; one out of every ten Mexican nationals resides in the United States...the vast majority illegally.

Since Mexifornia appeared, the debate no longer splits along liberal/conservative, Republican/Democrat, or even white/brown fault lines. Instead, class consider-ations more often divide Americans on the issue. The ma-jority of middle-class and poor Whites, Asians, African-Americans, and Hispanics wish to close the borders. They see few advantages to cheap service labor, since they are not so likely to need someone to mow their lawns, watch their kids, or clean their houses. Because the less well off eat out less often, use hotels infrequently, and don't periodically remodel their homes, the advantages to the economy of inexpensive, off-the-books illegal-alien labor are not so apparent.

But the downside surely is apparent. Truck drivers, car-penters, janitors, and gardeners, unlike lawyers, doc-tors, actors, writers, and professors...correctly feel that their jobs are threatened, or at least their wages lowered, by cheaper rival workers from Oaxaca or Jalisco. And Americans who live in communities where thousands of illegal aliens have arrived en masse are more likely to lack the money to move when Spanish-speaking students flood the schools and gangs proliferate. Poorer Americans of all ethnic backgrounds take for granted that poverty provides no exemption from mastering English, so they wonder why the same is not true for incoming Mexican nationals. Less than a mile from Victor's home is a for-mer farmhouse whose new owner moved in several sta-tionary Winnebagos, propane tanks, and outdoor cook-ing facilities...and apparently four or five entire families rent such facilities right outside his back door. Dozens live where a single family used to...a common sight in rural California that reifies illegal immigration in a way that books and essays cannot.

The problem is that laws originally intended to ensure a veneer (admittedly thin) of civilization over innate chaos are being ignored...in the interest of political correctness. Roads are filled with drivers who have passed a "minimum" test to ensure that they are not a threat to others. Single-family residential zoning laws to ensure that there is adequate sewer, garbage, and water services for all, go un-enforced. Periodic county inspections to ensure that un-tethered dogs are licensed and free of disease and that housing is wired and plumbed properly to prevent mayhem are a thing of the past. What about a consensus on school taxes to ensure that there are enough teachers and classrooms for such sudden spikes in student populations? The state now just appears to be unwilling to enforce all the above inspection and zoning regulations in these growing enclaves...even spurning those laws and regulation.

All these now-neglected or forgotten rules and regulations are proving costly to the taxpayers. In Victor's own experience, the slow progress made in rural California since the 1950s of his youth...in which the county inspected their farm's rural dwellings, eliminated the once-ubiquitous rural outhouses, shut down substandard housing, and fined violators in hopes of providing a uniform humane standard of residence for all rural residents... has been abandoned in just a few years of laissez-faire policy toward illegal aliens. His neighborhood is reverting to conditions more common to the 1950, but with the insult of far higher tax rates added to the injury of nonexistent enforcement of once-comprehensive statutes. The government's attitude at all levels is to punish the dutiful citizen's misdemeanors while ignoring the alien's felonies, on the logic that the former will at least comply while the latter either cannot or will not.

Fairness about who is allowed into the United States is another issue that reflects class divides...especially since almost 70 percent of all immigrants, legal and illegal, arrive from Mexico. Asians, for example, are puzzled as to why their relatives wait years for official approval to enter the United States, while Mexican nationals come across the border illegally, counting on serial amnesties to obtain citizenship.

These class divisions cut both ways, and that helps explain the mandarins echoing the arguments of the elite Chicano studies professors. Both tend to ridicule the far less affluent Minutemen and English-only activists, in part because they do not experience firsthand the problems associated with illegal immigration but instead find millions of aliens grist for their own contrasting agendas. Indeed, every time an alien crosses the border legally, fluent in English and with a high school diploma, the La Raza industry and the corporate farm or construction company most likely lose a constituent.

The ripples of September 11, whether seen in the arrests of dozens of potential saboteurs here in America or the terrorist bombings abroad in Madrid and London, Americans should be reminded that our enemies can only do us harm if they can first, somehow, enter the United States. Again, it makes little sense to screen tourists, inspect cargo containers, and check the passenger lists of incoming flights, when our border with an untrustworthy Mexico remains porous. While it may be true that the opponents of illegal immigration have used the post–September 11 fear, of terrorism, to further their own agenda of closing the border with Mexico, they are absolutely correct that presently the best way for jihadist cells to cross into the United States is overland from the south.

Other foreign developments have also steered the debate ever more rightward. In the last decade, the United States has clearly seen the wages of sectarianism and ethnic chauvinism abroad. Why then, when we are spending blood and money abroad to encourage the melting pot and national unity, would anyone wish to contribute to tribalism or foster the roots of such ethnic separatism here in the United States?

Moreover, all during the 1990s, blue-state America offered up the European Union as the proper postmodern antidote to the United States. But just as we have recoiled from the European Union's "statist" and undemocratic tendencies, which have resulted in popular dissatisfaction, sluggish economic growth, high unemployment, falling demography, and unsustainable entitlement commitments...even as its unassimilated Muslim minorities serves as another canary in the mine. The riots in France, the support for jihadism among Pakistanis in London, and the demands of Islamists in Scandinavia, Germany, and the Netherlands do not encourage Americans to let in more poor Mexican illegal immigrants with loud agendas, or to embrace the multicultural salad bowl over their own distinctive melting pot.

Then there were the April–May 2006 demonstrations here in the United States, when nearly half a million protesters took to the streets of our largest cities, from Chicago to Los Angeles. Previously, naive Americans had considered that their own discussions over border security and immigration were in their own hands. And while Chicano-rights organizations and employer lobbyists were often vehement in their efforts to keep the border open, illegal aliens themselves used to be mostly quiet about our internal legal debates.

This spring Americans witnessed millions of illegal aliens who were not only unapologetic about their illegal status but were demanding that their host accommodate their own political grievances, from providing driver's licenses to full amnesty. The largest demonstrations...held on May Day, with thousands of protesters waving Mexican flags and bearing placards depicting the communist insurrectionist Che Guevara, only confirmed to most Americans that illegal immigration was out of control and beginning to become politicized along the lines of Latin American radicalism. Victor chronicled in Mexifornia the anomaly of angry protesters waving the flag of the country they vehemently did not wish to return to, and now the evening news beamed these images to millions. In short, the radical socialism of Latin America, seething in the angry of millions who flocked to support Venezuela's Hugo Chávez, Bolivia's Evo Morales, and Mexico's Andrés López Obrador, had now seemingly been imported into our own largest cities.

Turmoil in areas of Mexico that send many illegal aliens to the United States is especially worrisome. Recently, for example, almost the entire state of Oaxaca was in near-open revolt over efforts to force the resignation of provincial governor Ulises Ruiz. There was widespread lawlessness, vigilantism, and at times the complete breakdown of order. All this feeds the growing perception that illegal aliens increasingly are arriving not merely as economic refugees, but as political dissidents who don't hesitate to take to the streets here to demand social justice, as they did back home.

More important still, Oaxaca's troubles cast doubt on the conventional wisdom that illegal immigration is a safety valve that allows Mexico critical time to get its house in order. Perhaps the opposite is true; some of the areas, like Oaxaca, that send the most illegal aliens to the United States, still experience the greatest social tensions...in part because of the familial disruption and social chaos that results when adult males flee and depopulated communities consequently become captive to foreign remittances.

Two other issues have persuaded Americans to close the borders, the attitude of the Mexican government and the problems with first-generation native-born children of illegal aliens.

Worker remittances sent back to Mexico now earn it precious American dollars equal to the revenue from 500,000 barrels of daily exported oil. In short, Mexico cannot afford to lose its second-largest source of hard currency and will do almost anything to ensure its continuance. When Mexico City publishes comic books advising its own citizens how best to cross the Rio Grande, Americans take offense. Not only does Mexico brazenly wish to undermine American law to subsidize its own failures, but it also assumes that those who flee northward are among its least educated, departing without much ability to read beyond the comic-book level.

We are learning that not only does Mexico want its expatriates to send cash back home, but also expects them to lobby for Mexican interests, once they are safely away from their motherland. We are discovering that Mexico doesn't have much concern about the welfare of its citizens abroad in America. The conservative estimate of $15 billion sent home will always come at the expense of low-paid Mexicans toiling here. They must live in impoverished circumstances if they are to send substantial portions of their wages home to Mexico. It also comes at the expense of American taxpayers, providing healthcare and food subsidies in efforts to offer a safety net to cash-strapped illegal aliens. So it is not just that Mexico exports its own citizens, but it does so on the expectation that they are serfs of a sort, who, like the helots of old, surrender much of the earnings of their toil to their distant masters.

But even more grotesquely, in the last five years, the Mexican real-estate market has boomed on the Baja California peninsula. Once Mexico grasped that its own unspoiled coast was highly desirable for wealthy expatriate Americans, as a continuation of the prized but crowded Santa Barbara and San Diego seaside corridor, it began to reform its real-estate market, making the necessary changes in property and title law. It then welcomed cash-laden subdivision builders looking to come south. This is sound economics, but examine the ethical message...Mexico City will send the United States millions of its own illiterate and poor whom it will neither feed nor provide with even modest housing, but at the same time it welcomes thousands of Americans with cash to build expensive seaside second homes.

Of course, the ultimate solution to the illegal immigration debacle is for Mexican society to bring itself up to the levels of affluence found in the United States by embracing market reforms of the sort we have seen in South Korea, Taiwan, and China. But rarely do Mexican supporters of such globalization, or their sympathetic counterparts in the United States, see the proliferation of a Wal-Mart or Starbucks down south in such terms. Rather, to them American consumerism and investment in Mexico suggest only an owed reciprocity of sentiment: Why should Americans get mad about Mexican illegals coming north when our own crass culture, with its blaring neon signs in English, spreads southward? In such morally equivalent arguments, it is never mentioned that Americanization occurs legally and brings capital, while Mexicanization comes about by illegal means and is driven by poverty.

At the same time, focus has turned more to the U.S.-born children of Mexican illegal immigrants, in whom illegitimacy, school dropout rates, and criminal activity have risen to such levels that we can longer simply dismiss Mexican immigration as resembling the more problematic but eventually successful Italian model of a century ago. Then, large numbers of southern European Catholics, most without capital or education, arrived en masse from Italy and Sicily, lived in ethnic enclaves, and for decades lagged behind the majority population in educational achievement, income, and avoidance of crime...before achieving financial parity as well as full assimilation and intermarriage. Since 1990, the number of poor Mexican-Americans has climbed 52 percent, a figure that skews U.S. poverty rates. Billions of dollars spent on our own poor will not improve our poverty statistics when 1 million of the world's poorest cross our border each year. The number of impoverished black children has dropped 17 percent in the last 16 years, but the number of Hispanic poor has gone up 43 percent. We don't like to talk of illegitimacy, but here again the ripples of illegal immigration reach the U.S.-born generation. Half of all births to Hispanic Americans have been illegitimate, 42 percent higher than the general rate of the American population. Illegitimacy is higher, in general, in Mexico than in the United States, but with the multipliers of illegal status, lack of English, and an absence of higher education added to the equation...the children of Mexican immigrants have illegitimacy rates even higher than those found in either Mexico or the United States.

Education levels reveal the same dismal pattern; nearly half of all Hispanics are not graduating from high school in four years. And the more Hispanic a school district becomes, the greater level of failure for Hispanic students. In the Los Angeles district, 73 percent Hispanic, 60 percent of the students are not graduating. But the real tragedy is that, of those Hispanics who do graduate, only about one in five will have completed a high school curriculum that qualifies for college enrollment. That partly helps to explain why at many campuses of the California State University system, almost half of the incoming class must first take remedial education. Less than 10 percent of those who identify themselves as Hispanic have graduated from college with a bachelor's degree. Victor found that teaching Latin to first-generation Mexican-Americans and illegal aliens was valuable not so much as an introduction to the ancient world but as their first experience with remedial English grammar.

Meanwhile, almost one in three Mexican-American males between the ages of 18 and 24 recently reported being arrested, one in five has been jailed, and 15,000 illegal aliens are currently in the California penal system.

Statistics like these have changed the debate radically. While politicians and academics assured the public that illegal aliens came here only to work and would quickly assume an American identity, the public's own ad hoc and empirical observations of vast problems with crime, illiteracy, and illegitimacy have now been confirmed by hard data.

Victor wrote that ever since the influx of illegals into his quiet valley became a flood, he has had five drivers leave the road, plow into his vineyard, and then abandon their cars without evidence of either registration or insurance. On each occasion, they simply walked or ran away from the scene of thousands of dollars in damage. Similarly, an intoxicated driver who ran a stop sign and hit his car broadside also fled the scene. Our farmhouse in the Central Valley has been broken into three times. We used to have an open yard; now it is walled, with steel gates on the driveway. Such anecdotes have become common occurrence in the American Southwest. Ridiculed by elites as evidence of prejudice, these stories, now supported by statistical studies...reflect the hard facts.

More than four years after Mexifornia first appeared in City Journal, the growing national discomfort over illegal immigration is not only apparent in the rightward shift of the debate, but also in the absence of any new arguments for open borders. While the old arguments, Americans are finally concluding, really do erode the law, reward the cynical here and abroad, and needlessly divide Americans along class, political, and ethnic lines.

CHAPTER 11

I was not familiar with this writer, but I found his article on why Detroit has fallen so far since its heydays, to be very intriguing. It's just another example that California's situation is not an isolated anomaly, but rather a growing common denominator.

This is a powerful message about the failure of the Great Society.

How in the world do we get out of this mess? This is a perfect example of how good intentions without adequate foresight can produce an absolute nightmare. Never underestimate the downside of human nature.

For 15 years, from the mid 1970s to 1990, I worked in Detroit, Michigan. I watched it descend into an abyss of crime, debauchery, gunplay, drugs, school truancy, car jacking, gangs and human depravity. I watched entire city blocks burned out. I watched graffiti explode on buildings, cars, trucks, buses and schoolyards. Trash was everywhere! Detroiters walked through it, tossed more into it and just ignored it.

Tens of thousands and then, hundreds of thousands today

exist on federal welfare, free housing and food stamps! With Aid to Dependent Children, minority women birthed eight to 10 and, in one case, one woman birthed 24 kids as reported by the Detroit Free Press...all on American taxpayer dollars. A new child meant a new car payment, new TV and whatever mom wanted. I saw Lyndon Baines Johnson's "Great Society" flourish in Detroit. If you give money for doing nothing, you will get more hands out to take money for doing nothing.

Mayor Coleman Young, perhaps the most corrupt mayor in America, outside of Richard Daley in Chicago, rode Detroit down to its knees. He set the benchmark for cronyism, incompetence and arrogance. As a black man, he said, "I am the MFIC." The IC meant in charge. You can figure out the rest. Detroit became a majority black city with 67 percent African-Americans.

As a United Van Lines truck driver for the summer, a math and science teacher during the school year, I loaded hundreds of American families into my van for a new life in another city or state. Detroit plummeted from 1.8 million citizens to 912,000 today. At the same time, legal and illegal immigrants converged on the city, so much so, that Muslims numbered over 300,000. Mexicans numbered 400,000 throughout Michigan, but most work in Detroit.

As the whites moved out, the Muslims moved in...and as the crimes became more violent, the whites fled. Finally, unlawful Mexicans moved in at a torrid pace. Detroit suffers so much shoplifting that grocery stores no longer operate in many inner city locations.

You could cut the racial tension in the air with a knife! Detroit may be one our best (extreme) examples of multiculturalism, pure dislike and total separation from America!

Today, you hear Muslim calls to worship over the city like a new American Baghdad with hundreds of Islamic mosques in Michigan, paid for by Saudi Arabia oil money. High school flunk out rates reached 76 percent last June according to NBC's Brian Williams. Classrooms resemble foreign countries more than America. English? Few speak it! The city features a 50 percent illiteracy rate and growing. Unemployment hit 28.9 percent in 2009 as the auto industry vacated the city.

In Time Magazine October 4, 2009, "The Tragedy of Detroit: How a great city fell and how it can rise again." I choked on the writer's description of what had happened.

"If Detroit had been savaged by a hurricane and submerged by a ravenous flood, we would know a lot more about it," said Daniel Okrent. "If drought and carelessness had spread brush fires across the city, we would see it on the evening news every night. Earthquake, tornadoes, you name it...if natural disaster had devastated the city that was once the living proof of American prosperity, the rest of the country might have taken notice.

But Detroit, once our fourth largest city, now 11th and slipping rapidly, has had no such luck. Its disaster has long been a slow unwinding that seemed to remove it from the rest of the country. Even the death rattle that in the past year emanated from its signature industry brought more attention to the auto executives than to the people of the city, who had for so long been victimized by their dreadful decision-making."

As Coleman Young's corruption brought the city to its knees, no amount of federal dollars could save the incredible payoffs, kickbacks and illegality permeating his administration. I witnessed the city's death from the seat of my 18-wheeler tractor-trailer because I moved people out of every sector of decaying Detroit.

"By any quantifiable standard, the city is on life support. Detroit's treasury is $300 million short of the funds needed to provide the barest municipal services," Okrent said. "The school system, which six years ago was compelled by the teachers' union, to reject a philanthropist's offer of $200 million to build 15 small, independent charter high schools, is currently in receivership. The murder rate is soaring, and 7 out of 10 remain unsolved. Three years after Katrina devastated New Orleans, unemployment in that city hit a peak of 11 percent. In Detroit, the unemployment rate is 28.9 percent. That's worth spelling out, twenty-eight point nine percent."

Detroit's story is not simply one about a great city's collapse; it's also about the erosion of the industries that helped build the country we know today. The ultimate fate of Detroit will reveal much about the character of America in the 21st century. If what was once the most prosperous manufacturing city in the nation has been brought to its knees, what does that say about our recent past? And if it can't find a way to get back up, what does that say about our future?

The auto industry will not be coming back to Detroit. Immigration will keep pouring more and more uneducated, third world immigrants from the Middle East into Detroit...thus creating a beachhead for Islamic hegemony in America. If the 50 percent illiteracy continues, we will see more homegrown terrorists spawned out of the Muslim ghettos of Detroit. Illiteracy plus Islam equals walking human bombs. You have already seen it in Madrid, Spain, London, England, and Paris, France with train and subway bombings and riots. As their numbers grow, so will their power to enact their barbaric Sharia Law that negates republican forms of government, first amendment rights and subjugates women to the lowest rungs on the human ladder. We will see more honor killings by upset husbands, fathers and brothers that demand subjugation by their daughters, sisters and wives. Muslims prefer to use beheadings of women to scare the hell out of any other members of their sect from straying.

Multiculturalism: once again, the perfect method to kill our language, culture, country and way of life.

By Frosty Wooldridge

Yet another example of how our immigration policies... or lack of, and our welfare/entitlement mentality are destroying America, as we knew it.

As the devil's advocate I'm compelled to ask, "Is it right for the habitual non-contributors to continue to have a say in how the contributors' money is redistributed?" It seems that we allow those who "work the system" rather than working a job, to have too much influence and too little accountability when it comes to "their" entitlements...their standard of living.

The Bible tells us, "the poor you will have always, help them when you can." Jesus was speaking to believers and not the government in his passage.

CHAPTER 12

Ahhhhhh, the union life!

Growing up as the neighbor of a union big shot, I learned at an early age who made the big bucks. I was disgusted when my neighbor would arrive home in his brand new, top-of-the-line car (a new one every year...and one for his wife also), his copious gold chains and expensive watches.

His wife would swish about with her designer clothes (well, in looking back from my perspective today...they looked like designer clothes), and like her husband...she was always weighted down with gold and silver. They seemed to take pleasure in describing their trips to exotic places for his meetings, and the lavish accommodations afforded them. That lifestyle was in sharp contrast to the one we lived.

My father was a veteran and a hard working blue-collar guy who always paid his union dues right on time. My mother also had to work and paid her dues as well. They belonged to the unions because, in order to work, they had to join.

So is it any wonder that I have always had a measure of disdain for unions to this day? They had their time, but times have changed. Wake up union workers. Where do you think your dues are going? Do you ready think the unions care about you as an individual?

The biggest myth about labor unions is that unions are for the workers. Unions are for unions, just as corporations are for corporations and politicians are for politicians.

Nothing shows the utter cynicism of the unions and the politicians who do their bidding, like the so-called "Employee Free Choice Act" that the Obama administration tried to push through Congress. Employees' free choice as to whether or not to join a union is precisely what that legislation would destroy.

Workers already have a free choice in secret-ballot elections conducted under existing laws. As more and more workers in the private sector have voted to reject having a union represent them, the unions' answer has been to take away secret-ballot elections.

Under the "Employee Free Choice Act," unions would not have to win in secret-ballot elections in order to represent the workers. Instead, union representatives could simply collect signatures from the workers until they had a majority.

Why do we have secret ballots in the first place, whether in elections for unions or elections for government officials? To prevent intimidation and allow people to vote how they want to, without fear of retaliation.

This is a crucial right that unions want to take away from workers. The actions of union mobs in Wisconsin, Ohio and elsewhere give us a free home demonstration of how little they respect the rights of those who disagree with them and how much they rely on harassment and threats to get what they want.

It takes world-class chutzpah to call circumventing secret ballots the "Employee Free Choice Act." To unions, workers are just the raw material used to create union power, just as iron ore is the raw material used by U.S. Steel and bauxite is the raw material used by the Aluminum Company of America.

The most fundamental fact about labor unions is that they do not create any wealth. They are one of a growing number of institutions that specialize in siphoning off wealth created by others, whether those others are businesses or the taxpayers.

There are limits to how long unions can siphon off money from businesses, without facing serious economic repercussions.

The most famous labor union leader, the legendary John L. Lewis, head of the United Mine Workers from 1920-to-1960, secured rising wages and job benefits for the coal miners, far beyond what they could have gotten out of a free market based on supply and demand.

But there is no free lunch: An economist at the University of Chicago once called John L. Lewis "the world's greatest oil salesman."

His strikes that interrupted the supply of coal, as well as the resulting wage increases that raised its price, caused many individuals and businesses to switch from using coal to using oil, leading to a reduction in the number of coal miners employed. The higher wage rates also led coal companies to replace many miners with machines.

The net result was a huge decline in employment in the

coal mining industry, leaving many mining towns virtually ghost towns by the 1960s. There is no free lunch.

Similar things happened in the unionized steel industry and in the unionized automobile industry. At one time, U.S. Steel was the largest steel producer in the world and General Motors the largest automobile manufacturer. But times have changed. Their unions were riding high in their heyday, but they too discovered that there is no free lunch, as their members lost jobs by the hundreds of thousands.

Workers have also learned that there is no free lunch, which is why they have, over the years, increasingly voted against being represented by unions in secret ballot elections.

One set of workers, however, remained largely immune to such repercussions. These are government workers represented by public sector unions.

While oil could replace coal, while U.S. Steel dropped from number one in the world to number ten, and Toyota could replace General Motors as the world's leading producer of cars, government is a monopoly. Nobody is likely to replace the federal or state bureaucracies, no matter how much money the unions drain from the taxpayers.

That is why government unions continue to thrive while private sector unions decline. Taxpayers provide their free lunch.

With all of the union strife in Wisconsin, Indiana and New Jersey, and indications of more to come, it might be time to shed a bit of light on unions as an economic unit.

First, let's get one important matter out of the way. I value freedom of association, and non-association, even in ways that are not always popular and often deemed despicable. I support a person's right to be a member or not be a member of a labor union. From my view, the only controversy regarding unions is what should they be permitted and not permitted to do.

According to the Department of Labor, most union members today work for state, local and federal government. Close to 40 percent of public employees are unionized. As such, they represent a powerful political force in elections. If you're a candidate for governor, mayor or city councilman, you surely want the votes and campaign contributions from public employee unions. In my view, that's no problem. The problem arises after you win office and sit down to bargain over the pay and working conditions with unions who voted for you.

Given the relationship between politicians and public employee unions, we should not be surprised that public employee wages and benefits often average 45 percent higher than their counterparts in the private sector. Frequently they receive pension and health care benefits making little or no contribution.

How is it that public employee unions have such a leg up on their private-sector brethren? The answer is not rocket science. Employers in the private sector have a bottom line. If they overcompensate their employees, company profits will sink. The company might even face bankruptcy.

Of course, if private companies can count on federal government bailouts, as did General Motors and Chrysler, they can maintain a comfy relationship with their unions. But no such bottom line exists in the government sector. Politicians have every reason to grant benefits to their political allies, in this case public employee unions. They don't pick up the tab; it's unorganized taxpayers who face higher taxes.

Wisconsin's Governor Scott Walker says that stripping the workers of collective bargaining rights, and limiting talks to the subject of basic wages, is necessary to give the state the flexibility to get its finances in order and spare taxpayers further grief.

Consider the cushy deal for many of California's unionized state and local police, fire and prison employees. They have what's called a "3 percent at 50" formula that determines their retirement check. It's based on 3 percent of the average of the three highest-paid years of the employee's career, multiplied by the number of years on the job. An employee with 20 years of service can retire at age 50 and receive 60 percent of his salary. Employees often boost their retirement income by putting in a lot of overtime hours during their last three years of service.

Temple University professor William Dunkelberg wrote in his recent CNBC article, "Should Unions Have the Power to Tax?" "The 'employers' (taxpayers through their elected officials) have slowly lost their ability to determine the terms of employment offers. The unions now determine working hours, hiring criteria, the quantity of 'output' to be produced per day, the number of sick, vacation and holiday days, how their performance will be evaluated, etc. No longer can the employer make an 'offer' for a job with requirements that fit the needs of the public institution."

While government jobs have been steadily increasing for decades, those numbers have jumped exponentially during the current administration..."far" out numbering hiring in the private sector for the same period.

Currently, approximately 16 percent of Americans work for the government...at some level. If we can assume their respective spouses will vote along with them, that voting block will balloon to near 32 percent. If/when it reaches 51 percent, the game is over and "we" lose.

Major states like California, New York, Illinois, Ohio and New Jersey...and the federal government, are on the verge of bankruptcy. Large cities like Los Angeles; Chicago; New York; Washington, D.C.; Newark; and Detroit are facing bankruptcy as well. Does that tell you something? It tells me that we can no longer afford to do what we've done in the past.

I just read in the newspaper today that the nation's largest teachers union voted to support President Barack Obama's 2012 re-election bid, making it one of the earliest union endorsements for the administration. About 72 percent of the National Education Association's representative assembly voted to recommend the president's candidacy to its 3.2 million members, despite past disagreements with the administration over elements of the president's education reform agenda.

Surprise, surprise...almost 18 months until the election and "they" don't even know who his challenger will be, but it matters not...Obama could be running against Jesus Christ and the union would still endorse him, because they own him...he's their man.

CHAPTER 13

S peaking of the President, I can still remember the
olden days, when life was less complicated...and my
mother telling me that anybody could become president.
She said that if I worked hard, lived a straightforward
and honorable life that even a young boy like me, from
nowhere...could reach the top. Well...she was right about
anyone being able to reach the top rung, but neglected
to add...even if for all the wrong reasons.

While I've done nothing but criticize the man, I failed to
take into consideration two things he has accomplished
during the first two years of his administration. First,
he and his administration have made Carter and his
administration appear competent. The second is that he
and his administration have made Nixon and his administration appear honest. Now, let's be honest ourselves...
who else could have done that?

The latest Social Security Trustees Report tells us that
the program will be insolvent by the year 2037. The combined un-funded liability of Social Security and Medicare
has reached nearly $107 trillion in today's dollars. That
is about seven times the size of the U.S. economy and
10 times the size of the national debt. Those entitlement

programs, along with others, account for nearly 60 percent of federal spending. They are what Congress calls non-discretionary spending. About half of discretionary spending is for national defense. Each year, non-discretionary spending consumes a higher and higher percentage of the federal budget.

The language Congress uses to describe their spending is corrupt beyond redemption. Think about the term entitlement. If one American is entitled to something he didn't earn, where in the world does Congress get the money? It's not Santa or the Tooth Fairy. The only way Congress can give one American a dollar is to first take it from another American. Therefore, an entitlement is a congressionally given right for one American to live at the expense of another. In other words, Congress forcibly uses one American to serve the purposes of another American. While it's certainly not an apple-to-apple comparison, it differs only by scale from that ugly part of our history where black people were forcibly used to serve the purposes of their slave masters.

What about the terms discretionary versus non-discretionary congressional spending? Non-discretionary refers to uncontrollable things like sunsets and sunrises, low tides and high tides and laws of thermodynamics. By contrast, all congressional spending is discretionary and controllable. For political expedience, Congress has written laws to shield certain spending from annual budget scrutiny by calling it non-discretionary.

The level of congressional spending is unsustainable, but how willing are Americans to do anything about it? A courageous member of Congress, Paul Ryan, R-Wisconsin, chairman of the House Budget Committee, has put forth a budget plan that would trim the deficit by $4.4 trillion over 10 years by "reforming" Medicare and Medicaid, making defense cuts and imposing hard spending caps on domestic spending.

Ryan's plan was immediately attacked as trying to balance the budget on the backs of the poor. In the wake of this attack, even some of his Republican backers, including House Speaker John Boehner, have become lukewarm in support.

The president and his supporters call for tax increases as a means to cover the deficit, but higher tax revenues cannot eliminate the deficit. Factoring in inflation, federal tax revenue today is 23 times greater than it was in 1960, but congressional spending is 42 times greater. During the last half-century, except for five years, the nation has faced a federal budget deficit. It's just simple math, if tax revenues soar, but congressional spending soars more, budget deficits cannot be avoided.

People ask what can be done to save our nation from decline. To ask that represents a misunderstanding of history and possibly a bit of arrogance. After all, how different are Americans from the Romans, Spaniards, French and the English? They were once mighty nations standing at the top of civilization. At the height of these nations's prosperity, no one would have predicted that they would become third-rate nations, especially England. If during Queen Victoria's Jubilee in 1887, anyone had suggested that England would become a third-rate nation and would later be challenged, on the high seas, by a sixth-rate nation (Argentina)...that person would have been shouted down as an idiot.

One chief causal factor for the decline of those former great nations is what has been described as "bread and circuses," where government spends money for the shallow and immediate wants of the population, and civic virtue all but disappears. For the past half-century, our nation has been doing precisely that...the same thing that brought other great nations down. We might have already reached the point of no return. If so, we deserve it.

The 2008 financial crash originated with a housing bubble. Not long ago, the cheap-money policies of the Federal Reserve, the infusion of trillions of dollars in new foreign investments and the misguided policies of Freddie Mac and Fannie Mae all conspired to extend, to millions of Americans, lots of easy cash for inflated houses that they could hardly afford. Owning a house was seen as a "right" rather than the just rewards of household sacrifice, delayed gratification and budgetary discipline.

Builders, lenders, realtors and bureaucrats all got in on the easy-money Ponzi scheme...until a few noticed that the emperor had no clothes and that pedestrian homes were rarely worth what unqualified purchasers had paid for them. Financial hysteria followed when shaky borrowers began to miss mortgage payments, walked away, and lenders panicked. The subsequent meltdown is history.

There is a similar pension bubble rising as well. There is perhaps as much as $6 trillion owed in retirement pledges to Americans, and up to an estimated $500 billion of that is on California's tab. That obligation, under present conditions, simply cannot be met. For the past 30 years, politicians, more eager for votes than for ensuring the payment of what they had promised...outbid each other to offer more lavish retirement packages to union members and public employees. A generous retirement package was considered a "right" rather than an investment predicated on past savings coupled with modest interest and dividends.

There may already be an immediate $1 trillion shortfall in meeting what is owed current retirees. Pensioners on the receiving end are becoming more numerous, older and more affluent, while the younger workers on the paying end are becoming less numerous and poorer. At some point, a city, a state or perhaps...even the Social Security system is going to announce that there is no more money. Then, if there isn't another financial crisis and Wall Street meltdown, the fantasy will end with workers paying higher contributions, retiring later and receiving less.

Then there is the higher education bubble; with its collective student debt nearing $1 trillion and no guarantees that it will be paid back. Lots of poor college students and their strapped parents are floating huge government-subsidized student loans to pay for ever more costly bachelor's degrees that no longer ensure that the recipients are either well-educated, will find a job upon graduation or if employed, will be better paid than the vocationally trained. Going to college has somehow become another "right" rather than a privilege predicated on superior academic achievement, financial sacrifice and continued academic discipline.

There are disturbing commonalities to these expanding bubbles...and others, like the recently enacted health care entitlement on the way. The rich and connected seem exempt from the impending reckoning. And the poor assume the government will offer them debt relief. Those in between are on their own and will have to pay more for receiving less.

America is not creating enough wealth to justify the notion that everyone should go to college, get a higher-paying job than their parents had, buy a nice, affordable house, and retire earlier...with more money than did prior generations.

We have forgotten what real wealth is...and how tenuous the good life is. Prosperity can only be created by education, and skilled workers who directly convert natural resources into commodities that improve and/or make life better. The nonproductive sector in government, law and banking must facilitate that process with efficient and transparent financial and political systems.

Instead, we are failing to provide our college graduates with unique skills that make them rare assets in the global competitive arena. Meanwhile, our more talented and better-trained workers are suing, subsidizing and regulating more than ever...instead of searching for more oil and gas, supplying more water to productive farmland, fast-tracking nuclear power plants, manufacturing machines and consumer goods, or devising new and more efficient ways to help others produce such things as food, fuel and additional tangible products. In other words, we are living the good life in the abstract that we have not quite earned in the concrete.

The United States is rapidly becoming the very first "post-industrial" nation on the globe. All great economic empires eventually become fat and lazy and squander the great wealth that their forefathers have left them, but the pace at which America is accomplishing this is absolutely amazing. It was America that was at the forefront of the industrial revolution. It was America that showed the world how to mass-produce everything from automobiles to televisions to airplanes. It was the great American manufacturing base that crushed Germany and Japan in World War II.

But now we are witnessing the de-industrialization of America. Tens of thousands of factories have left the United States in the past decade alone. Millions upon millions of manufacturing jobs have been lost in the same time period. The United States has become a nation that consumes everything in sight and yet produces increasingly little.

Do you know what our biggest export is today? Waste paper. Yes, trash is the number one thing that we ship out to the rest of the world as we voraciously blow our money on whatever the rest of the world wants to sell to us. The United States has become bloated and spoiled and our economy is now just a shadow of what it once was. Once upon a time America could literally out produce the rest of the world combined. Today that is no longer true, but Americans sure do consume more than anyone else in the world. If the de-industrialization of America continues at this current pace, what possible kind of a future are we going to be leaving to our children?

Throughout history, great nations have been great at producing things. So if the United States continues to allow its manufacturing base to erode at such a staggering pace, how in the world can the United States continue to consider itself to be a great nation? We have created the biggest debt bubble in the history of the world in an effort to maintain a very high standard of living, but the current state of affairs is not anywhere close to sustainable. Every single month America goes deeper into debt and every single month America becomes poorer.

America is a naturally rich country, and unlike Russia, China, Egypt or Greece, we are "currently" stable, transparent, tolerant and free of civil strife. The result is that we are not doomed to see these bubbles expand and burst with the attendant social unrest. We need only return to our old American creed that wealth is created only with hard work and delayed gratification.

America must get back to producing real, rather than imaginary riches...and ignore the pleasing rhetoric that masks life's unpleasant realities.

An add to my earlier reference to the recently enacted health care "entitlement":

The American people should already know that Obama's plan to lower health costs while expanding coverage and bureaucracy is a myth, a promise of something that never was and never can be: "A bureaucracy lowering costs in a free society." Either the costs go up or the free society goes away; "A historical truth."

CHAPTER 14

"America will never be destroyed from the outside. If we falter and lose our freedoms, it will be because we destroyed ourselves."

Abraham Lincoln

The opening stages of the 2012 election campaign have begun. Some early salvos revolve around Republican Representative Paul Ryan's budget proposal and what to do about entitlements. President Barack Obama has shifted into campaign mode, and Republican contenders are lining up for a chance to challenge him. By all accounts, it will be a hard fought election. It will also be a testament to the increasing problems facing our election process. Problems that, if left unresolved, could lead to the dissolution of our Republic within the lifetime of many of those living today.

If that sounds alarmist or impossible to you, it shouldn't. No government in history has ever remained in the same form since the very creation of societies. In 1787, Alexander Tyler, a Scottish history professor, wrote, "A democracy is always temporary in nature; it simply cannot exist as a permanent form of government. A democracy will continue to exist up until the time that voters discover that they can vote themselves generous gifts from the public treasury. From that moment on, the majority always votes for the candidates who promise the most benefits from the public coffers, with the result that every democracy will finally collapse due to loose fiscal policy."

If that doesn't sound familiar, it should. In 2010, California voters returned to office the very legislators who are plunging the state ever deeper into debt. For good measure, they reelected U.S. Senator Barbara Boxer and sent a Democrat (well known for his liberalism) into the governor's office once again.

When our founders set up our Republic, they feared this very phenomenon. Thomas Jefferson wrote, "A democracy is nothing more than mob rule, where 51 percent of the people may take away the rights of the other 49 percent." They did everything they could to try to prevent this from happening.

Remember, in the original Constitution, U.S. senators weren't selected by popular vote. It is also why the founders set up the Electoral College to determine the election of the president. In today's politically correct climate, these men would be branded as elitist snobs; however, they were shrewd observers of human nature.

What they didn't have was a crystal ball. While they allowed for the growth of the United States...it is unlikely that most, if any, truly understood just how big the United States would become. In the first Congress, there were 91 lawmakers in both houses, less than we have in just the Senate today. Anyone who has served on jury duty knows how hard it is to get 12 people to agree. Obviously, this bogs down the legislative process.

The other unforeseen consequence was the effect this would have on the Electoral College that the founders had hoped would mitigate straight majority rule. In the first election, the biggest state had 12 electoral votes and the smallest had three. In 2012, the biggest state will have 55 votes while the smallest still has only three. The result is that big states are targeted and valued by candidates much more than small states, increasing the influence of the majority voters in these big states, something our founders had feared and tried to prevent.

The obvious solution would be to cut the Senate in half and trim the number of representatives to something more in line with the original 4-to-1 ratio, giving smaller states more say so in our Republic. Of course, that's not going to happen. Few, if any, politicians are going to legislate themselves out of a job.

Two other factors of our modern society were also unforeseen by our 18th century founders. They did not anticipate the pervasiveness of our modern media and the bias that has grown in what was supposed to be an impartial system of reporting the news. In modern elections, the side with the most money can flood the airways with partisan messages that can sway public opinion significantly. While such ads do not attempt to be fair, they are still very effective.

The troubling truth is that today's media bias was once the more impartial, hard news. While both sides claim bias, it should be clear the bias leans heavily left. The Center for Media and Public Affairs found that in 2008, 68 percent of news stories were favorable toward Barack Obama and 36 percent were favorable to John McCain.

Perception is also swayed by the media. President George W. Bush was perceived as a moron, and was ridiculed because he mispronounced "nuclear." President Obama is portrayed as the most intelligent president in our history in spite of his unwillingness to release his college transcripts, his consistent misuse of adjectives and adverbs and the tough time he has stringing a sentence together off the teleprompter. When he totally mispronounced "corpsman," it was no big deal as far as the media was concerned. He was just given a pass.

Alan Greenspan recently spoke at a gathering of financial investors and economists and delivered a politically incorrect observation: He verbalized, what most of us older generations already knew...that the younger, incoming generations are unprofessional, unprepared and unmotivated to fill the huge void being created as the baby-boomers are heading into retirement.

Okay, so maybe he didn't actually use the word "unmotivated," (that's just what I think) but he did say "unprepared." And he didn't say they were unprepared because of their progressive schooling, but I'm saying it is a big part of their "unpreparedness."

Way too many are living in, and addicted to...an imaginary techno world where life revolves around social networking, entitlements and other government granted "rights." In an environment such as that, I can understand why the baby-boomer's work ethic is falling by the wayside. It's just another relic from the past...old school, so passé.

Below is another example of how today's entitlement and it's my right mentality has distorted the values that made America the greatest country in the world.

Front page of my local newspaper:

College students in California have been complaining and even demonstrating (we seem to have more and more demonstrating in America today) because their

California State University tuitions have been increased. They became disgruntled at being required to assist more in paying for their education. Well, they can just get in line behind retired teachers, cops, firefighters, government officials, all illegal aliens, welfare and food stamp recipients, environmentalists, La Raza, the ACLU, and everyone else who accuses working Americans of not having deep-enough pockets.

They argue that it's not fair (we hear that a lot today) and that they are being punished for wanting to pursue an education (sounds like a politician's self-serving spin). Sorry kids, and I mean kids! You sound immature, very self-centered and actually like a bunch of entitlement-minded spoiled brats with lousy perspectives. I wonder how these folks feel about students in kindergarten through the 12th grade that don't pay a dime, plus free food, tutoring and day care billed to the taxpayer for 13-plus-years?

College is a free choice, not a Constitutional right.

Same day newspaper; 4 pages back:

A picture of Marine Lance Corporal Norberto Mendez, 22, his wife Lorena, and their two young sons. Lance Corporal Norberto Mendez was killed in Afghanistan last Sunday.

I wonder where his death rates on the fairness scale.

While the founding fathers were very intuitive about human nature and the gullibility of the trusting, they could never have envisioned the many misdirection paths America would traverse to reach this tipping point.

The upcoming election and the campaign leading up to it may show how rapidly we are approaching the prophetic words of Abraham Lincoln. "Our Republic is in peril. I fear the tipping point may already have been reached."

CHAPTER 15

It never fails. People are losing their jobs, or their mortgages are being foreclosed or can't afford health care, so the bright idea of the moment is for the government to take other peoples' money to make new jobs, bail out foreclosures and subsidize health care.

What's wrong with this picture?

College students yelp that their tuition at public schools has increased. Oh woe! Taxpayers need to step up to the plate and fork over some more of their dollars to subsidize the cost of education. Why, after all, should the ones being educated pay for their own education?

Notice that all the knee-jerk solutions involve keeping the price the same for the things that can no longer be afforded?

Guess what. That solution eventually runs into Margaret Thatcher's truism: "They will always run out of other people's money."

You've heard the very true complaint that reducing how much government pays doctors to treat Medicare patients will result in doctors leaving the practice of medicine. This is no doubt true, but only because doctors, like students, homeowners, workers and the rest of us have become accustomed to the singular solution...and that is, more of other peoples' money to subsidize what we want.

Here's how to break the otherwise never-ending-upward spiral of increasing costs and increasing tax subsidies.

Everyone works for less. That means college teachers, bank loan officers, doctors and workers across the spectrum. Labor is the primary cost of just about every aspect of the economy.

The only way to bring prices back to earth is to quit feeding the inflationary price machine. When doctors finally agree to work for 60 percent of what they are paid now, the cost of what they do will drop 40 percent. Not before.

The first impediment is that everyone is resistant to getting less then they were getting before.

But here's the larger impediment: Government subsidies. When they are entirely removed for college students, colleges will drop their prices to what the genuine market demand is by students who must pay their own way. That, of course, means college professors will be paid only as much as that amount of income can justify.

Along the way we will discover how much of everything is over-inflated in price and how much of that stuff we really would just as soon not buy if we have to use our own money, particularly if our own wages have been cut.

California houses aren't really worth $500,000 -to- $700,000...if Californians had to buy them earning 60 percent of their current wages.

Yeah, you're right. That "ain't" going to happen any time soon. But it may eventually happen on its own, in no small part because of Thatcher's truism. At some point, "we will run out of other people's money."

The option to voluntarily agreeing to live on less and consequently to spend less, thereby providing less to those who sell to us is that…"economic reality will do this for us, if we don't."

We see this with the stock market to a slight degree. Stocks rise, and then fall, as their perceived value falls. When jobs, commodities and services are allowed to rise and fall similarly, we can approach economic stability. That means cut out the government money that drives up the costs of education, health, housing and everything else.

By the way, that means the government won't need 40 percent of the money it collects now. And that means everyone whose salary is reduced will have a good chunk of the reduction offset by his or her tax cuts. And who knows, government might learn to live on less too.

And with that said, perhaps we wouldn't be struggling from year-to-year with a debt ceiling quagmire. Driven by opposing government subsidies, pork programs, entitlements, rights, financial support (at some level) for half the countries in the world, and far too many to enumerate… "cultural" programs that should be privately sponsored.

We've all heard the old Reaganism:

Government's view of the economy could be summed up in a few short phrases:

If it moves, tax it.

If it keeps moving, regulate it.

And if it stops moving,

Subsidize it.

There is something surreal and unnerving about our so-called "debt ceiling" negotiations staggering on in Washington. In the real world, negotiations on an increase in one's debt limit are conducted between the borrower and the lender. Only in Washington is a debt increase negotiated between two groups of borrowers.

Actually, it's more accurate to call them two groups of spenders. On the one side are Obama and the Democrats, who in a negotiation supposedly intended to reduce American indebtedness, are (surprise!) proposing massive increases in spending (an extra $33 billion for Pell College Grants, for example). The Democrat position is: You guys always complain that we spend, spend and spend like there's (what's the phrase again?) no tomorrow. So with that said, we're now proposing to spend, spend, spend and spend like there's no this evening.

On the other side are the Republicans, who are the closest anybody gets to representing, albeit somewhat tentatively and certainly less than forcefully, the actual borrowers...that's to say, you and your children and grandchildren. But in essence the spenders are negotiating among themselves how much debt they're going to burden you with. It's like you and your missus announcing that you've re-set your credit card limit to $1.3 million, and then telling the bank to send demands for repayment to Mr. and Mrs. Smith's kindergartner next door.

Nothing good is going to come from these ludicrously protracted negotiations over laughably meaningless accounting sleights-of-hand budget cuts...scheduled to kick in circa 2020. All the charade does is confirm to prudent analysts around the world that the depraved ruling class of the United States cannot self-correct, and, indeed, has no desire to.

When the 44th president took office, he made a decision that it was time for the already unsustainable levels of government spending...to finally break the bounds of reality, and frolic and gamble in the magical fairy kingdom of "Spendaholica." This year, the federal government borrows 43 cents of every dollar it spends, a ratio that is unprecedented. Barack Obama would like this to be, as they say, "the new normal"...at least until that 43 cents creeps up a nickel or so, or until the United States Government is spending twice as much it takes in, year in, year out, now and forever. If the Republicans refuse to go along with that, well, then the negotiations will collapse and, as he told Scott Pelley on CBS the other night, "Gran'ma gets it. Those monthly Social Security checks...I cannot guarantee that those checks will go out on August 3rd if we haven't resolved this issue," declared the president. "Because there may simply not be enough money in the coffers to do it."

But hang on. I thought the Social Security checks came out of the famous "Social Security trust fund," whose "trustees" assure us there's currently $2.6 trillion in there. Which should be enough for the August 3rd check run, shouldn't it? Golly, to listen to the president, you would almost get the impression that, by the time they saw the padlock off the old Social Security lockbox, there will be nothing in there but some yellowing IOUs and a few moths. Indeed, to listen to Obama, one might easily conclude that the whole rotten stinking edifice of federal government is an accounting trick. And that can't possibly be so, can it?

For the Most Gifted Orator in Human History, the president these days speaks largely in clichés, most of which he doesn't seem to be quite on top of. "Eric, don't call my bluff," he sternly reprimanded the GOP's Eric Cantor. Usually, if you're bluffing, the trick is not to announce it upfront. But, in fact, in his threat to have Granny eating dog food by Labor Day, Obama was calling his own bluff. The giant bluff against our future...government spending.

How many of "the wealthy" does it require to cover a one-and-a-half trillion-dollar shortfall every single year? When you need this big a fix, there aren't enough people to stick it to. "We are not broke," insists Van Jones, Obama's former "green jobs" czar and bespoke communist. "We were robbed, we were robbed. And somebody has our money!"

That somebody who has all our money is the government. They waste it on self-aggrandizing ideologue nitwits like Van Jones and his "green jobs" racket. How's the green jobs scene in your town? Going gangbusters, is it? Every day these guys burn through so much money that we'll never be able to bridge the gap. By that, I don't mean that when our government raises two trillion dollars...and then spends four trillion, that it's outspending America; I mean that it's outspending the planet.

Financing the United States' Debt, is there enough money in the world, and at what cost?

Yes, technically, there is enough money in the world...in the sense that, on current projections, by 2020 all it will take to finance the Government of the United States is for the rest of the planet to be willing to sink 19 percent of its GDP (Gross Domestic Product) into the United States' Treasury debt. Which we are being told is technically doable. Yeah, in the same sense that me dating Scarlett Johannson is technically doable.

Unfortunately, neither Scarlett nor the rest of the planet is willing to do either. It's not 2020, and we're not yet asking the rest of the planet for a fifth of its GDP. But already the world is imposing its own debt ceiling. Most of the debt issued by the Treasury so far this year has been borrowed from the Federal Reserve. That adds another absurd wrinkle to the D.C. charade: Washington is negotiating with itself over how much money to lend itself.

Meanwhile, the World's Greatest Orator bemoans the "intransigence" of Republicans. OK, what's your plan? Give us one actual program you're willing to cut, right now. Oh, don't worry, says Barack Obluffer. To demonstrate how serious he is, he has offered to put on the table, for fiscal year 2012, spending cuts of (stand well back now) $2 billion. That would be a lot in, say, Iceland or even Australia. Once upon a time it would have been a lot even in Washington. But today, $2 billion is what the "brokest" nation in history borrows every 10 hours. In other words, in less time than he spent sitting across the table negotiating his $2 billion cut, he borrowed it all back. A negotiation with Obama is literally not worth the time.

In order to fund Obamacare and the other opiates of Big Government dependency, the feds need to take 25 percent of our GDP now and forever. The "new normal." It can't be done. Look around you. The new normal is already here; flat-line jobs market, negative equity, and the dead parrot economy. What comes next will be profoundly abnormal.

Ozymandias:

And on the pedestal these words appear:

My name is Ozymandias, king of kings.

Look on my works, ye Mighty, and despair!

Nothing beside remains. Round the decay

Of that colossal wreck, boundless and bare

The lone and level sands stretch far away.

Percy Bysshe Shelley

This trope describes none other than the hubris of humankind itself. Humankind, being the self-centered species it is, has a tendency to think that the world revolves around them, and that they at their current time period have reached the true apex of civilization, the pinnacle of culture. In celebration of their glory, humanity builds monuments to itself. Architecture becomes grandiose, Crystal Spires and Togas become the hot new fashion trend, and pomp and splendor reign throughout the land. This is the pride before the fall.

On a smaller scale, however, this can also mean any work of fiction involving a cautionary tale where people blindly build or otherwise invest huge amounts of energy into a pursuit, confident that they will succeed, only to have it backfire, and end in catastrophe.

In the end, nothing is left but ashes and the ruins of a great effort gone to waste. Humanity learns a painful lesson. How The Mighty Have Fallen! At least for a while. As a trope in literature, this oftentimes comes up as an Aesop fable about Pride and Humility, and dating back to even Old Testament tales about the Tower of Babel, it is very much Older Than Dirt.

I wonder, do they still teach Shelley in high school; or just the "diversity manual" about "social justice" that the Omaha Public Schools paid for with $130,000 of "stimulus" funding?

CHAPTER 16

President Obama is demanding a big long-term budget deal. He won't sign anything less, he warns, asking, "If not now, then when?"

How about last December, when he ignored his own debt commission's recommendations? How about February, when he presented a budget that increases debt by $10 trillion over the next decade? How about April, when he sought a debt-ceiling increase with zero debt reduction attached?

Now, all of a sudden he's a born-again budget balancer prepared to bravely take on his own party by making deep cuts in entitlements. Really? Name one. He's been saying forever that he's prepared to discuss, engage, and converse about entitlement cuts. But never once has he publicly proposed a single structural change to any entitlement.

Hasn't the White House leaked that he's prepared to rise the Medicare age and/or change the cost-of-living calculation?

Anonymous talk is cheap. Leaks are designed to manipulate. Offers are floated and disappear.

Just say it, Mr. President. Give us one single structural change in entitlements...in public.

Unfortunately, the president is disingenuous in many areas. In support of his call for higher taxes combined with spending cuts, he cited Ronald Reagan's actions in 1982 in agreeing to a combination of tax increases and spending cuts. But he did not note that Reagan later regretted the deal because while all the tax increases were imposed...very few of the spending cuts were implemented, something the former Reagan communications director, Pat Buchanan, has been pointing out on the talk shows.

The president backed a budget bill by the Democratic-controlled Senate that would increase taxes while reducing some spending. But as he noted, the spending cuts mostly would be delayed. Which means the cuts could be canceled by a future Congress, just as happened to the illusory cuts promised to the "Gipper" nearly three decades ago.

In his call for compromise, Mr. Obama quoted the founder of the Democratic Party, Thomas Jefferson, who said, "Every man cannot have his way in all things." True, but he also should have cited this quote from the Sage of Monticello, "We must not let our rulers load us with perpetual debt. Taxation follows that, and in its train wretchedness and oppression."

It's the president who needs to compromise. Americans already are taxed enough. The spending binge of the past decade must be ended, and reversed.

But compromise for the president means, "I tell you what I want, and you give it to me." And his take on a balanced budget is, "We spend...and you pay more."

As part of his pose as the forward-looking grown-up...rising above all the others who play politics, Obama insists upon a long-term deal. And what is Obama's definition of long-term? Surprise: An agreement that gets him past November 6, 2012.

Nothing could be more political. It's like his Afghan surge wind-down date. September 2012 has no relationship to any military reality on the ground. It is designed solely to position Obama favorably going into the last weeks of his re-election campaign.

Yet the Olympian above-the-fray, no-politics-here pose, is succeeding. A pliant press swallows the White House story line, the great compromiser ("clearly exasperated," sympathized a Washington Post news story) being stymied by Republican "intransigence." The same words were later used in another front-page Post news story to describe the Republican position on taxes.

The memo having been established, Republicans have been neatly set up to take the fall if a deal is not reached by August 2nd. Obama is already waving the red flag, warning ominously that Social Security, disabled veterans' benefits, "critical" medical research, food inspection... without which agriculture shuts down, are in jeopardy.

With the Obama media leading the charge, the Republicans are being totally outmaneuvered.

But by what crazy calculation should Republicans allow themselves to be blamed for a debt crisis that could destabilize the economy and even precipitate a double-dip recession? Right now, Obama owns the economy and its 9.2 percent unemployment, 1.9 percent GDP growth and exploding debt about which he's done nothing. So why bail him out by sharing ownership?

Many years ago, 'someone' said, "If you didn't invite me to the big take-off, don't invite me to the crash landing."

If conservatives really want to get the nation's spending under control, the only way is to win the back the presidency. Put the question to the country and let the people decide. To seriously jeopardize the election now in pursuit of a long-term, small-government, Ryan-like reform, which is inherently unreachable without control of the White House, may be good for the soul; but it could very well devastate the bigger principle.

In Europe, austerity is in the air, and in the headlines: "Italy Fast-Tracks Austerity Vote." "Greek Minister Urges Austerity Consensus." "Portugal To Speed Austerity Measures." "Even the Queen Faces Funding Squeeze In Austerity Britain." The word has become so instantly ubiquitous that "Leftie" deadbeats are already opposed to it: "Austerity Protest Takes Place In Dublin." It can't be long now before old grizzled rockers are organizing some all-star Rockers Against Austerity gala.

By contrast, nobody seems ready to speed austerity measures through over here. "That word" isn't a component of the conversation...even though we're broke on a scale way beyond what Ireland or Portugal could ever dream of.

The problem is structural: There are not enough people doing enough work for enough of their lives. Developed nations have 30-year-old students and 50-year old retirees, and they wonder why the math doesn't add up.

By the way, demographically speaking, these categories... "adolescents" and "retirees" are an invention of our own time; they didn't exist a century ago. You were a kid until 13 or so, then you worked...and then you died.

In theory these structural problems can be fixed. But,

when you look at the nature of them, you have to wonder whether that will ever happen this side of a communal collapse. The ruling party in Washington is wedded to the principle that an 80-year-old social program is unchallengeable.

But "political reality" operates on different rules than routine reality. Thus, the "debt ceiling" debate is regarded by most Democrats and a few Republicans...as some sort of ghastly faux pas by boorish conservatives. Everyone knows the old debt-limit vote is merely a bit of traditional ceremony. You hit the debt ceiling, you just jack it up a couple trillion, and life goes on...or so it did until these GOP yahoos came along and decided to treat the vote as if it actually meant something.

Obama has done his best to pretend to take them seriously. He claimed to have a $4 trillion deficit-reduction plan. The court eunuchs of the press corps were impressed, and went off to file pieces hailing the president as the grown-up in the room. There was, in fact, no plan. No plan at all.

How about Harry Reid, the Senate Majority Leader? Has he got a plan? No. The Democratic Senator has shown no interest in producing a budget for two-and-a-half years. Unlike the president, Senator Reid can't even be bothered pretending he's interested in spending reductions. But he is interested in spending, and if that's your bag...then boring things like budgets only get in the way.

Don't worry...it's coming. The domestic media coverage of this story has been almost laughably fraudulent. To the court eunuchs, a failure to raise the debt ceiling by a couple of trillion dollars would signal to the world that America's government is embarrassingly dysfunctional. In reality, raising the debt ceiling by a couple of trillion, without any spending cuts…would confirm to the world that America's government is terminally dysfunctional.

In the debt-ridden treasuries of Europe, they're talking austerity. In the debt-ridden treasury of Washington, they're talking about more spending; Kathleen Sebelius is touting a new women's health program to be made available "without cost."

A half-century after the advent of the pill, the Obama administration is ushering in a change in women's health care potentially just as transformative: Coverage of birth control pills as prevention, and "morning-after pills" for the irresponsible…with no co-pays!

"Since birth control is the most common drug prescribed for women, health plans should make sure it's readily available," said Health and Human Services Secretary Kathleen Sebelius. "Not doing it would be like not covering flu shots."

Interesting rationale, comparing pregnancy to the flu… seems like quite a stretch to me.

And since prevention of unintended pregnancies is essential for the psychological, emotional and physical health of women (according to the dean of public health at UCLA), the rest of us are responsible for seeing that their lack of accountability doesn't affect their mental well-being.

And in the interest of "redistribution"…and entitlements, we will all be "required" to pay higher premiums for our health insurance.

At the risk of settling the superiority between a louse and a flea, I think Europe's political discourse is marginally less deranged than ours. The president is said to be the adult in the room because he is reported to be in favor of rising the age of Medicare eligibility from 65 to 67.

If that's the best offer, we're headed for real problems. As the Europeans are beginning to grasp, eventually political reality will collide with real reality.

More than 400 years ago, William Shakespeare wrote a riveting tragedy about a young, charismatic Danish prince who vowed to do the right thing in avenging his murdered father. That soon proved easier said than done. As a result, Hamlet couldn't quite ever act in time...given all the ambiguities that such a sensitive prince first had to sort out. In the meantime, a lot of bodies piled up through his indecision and hesitancy.

President Obama wanted to give us all universal health care. But then he discovered that the country was broke and that most people did not like his massive federal takeover. So we got both his health care, and so far... more than 1,000 exemptions from his landmark plan for unions, corporations and entire states.

Having taught most of his life, Obama is now finding out, as did Prince Hamlet, that thinking out every possible side of a question can mean never acting on any of them. And that worrying about pleasing everyone ensures pleasing no one.

The president wished to please his liberal supporters with more government "redistributive" programs and higher taxes on the wealthy. But such entitlements cost lots of money, more than $4 trillion in new borrowing in just three years...and scare to death the job-creating private sector.

So the president not only borrows at record levels, but also sets up a commission to warn us that his borrowing will soon bankrupt the country. He damns the "fat cat bankers" and the rich who "at some point" have made enough money, even as he courts them for campaign donations and begs their companies to start hiring new employees.

Obama warned us that we could not drill our way out of the ongoing gas crisis and needed instead to develop new green energy. As proof, he borrowed billions to promote wind and solar power, and stopped most new leases for fossil fuel exploration in Alaska, the West and offshore. But it turned out that we still need lots of oil as gas nears $4 a gallon. So the president brags that America is now pumping more oil under his green administration than ever before...but neglects to mention that it's true only because Presidents Clinton and Bush long ago approved the sort of oil leases that Obama had rejected.

President Obama wanted so much to discontinue George W. Bush's war on terror that he banned the phrase "war on terror" altogether. He apologized to the Muslim world, promised to "reset" our foreign policy, and vowed to close Guantanamo Bay and stop the other nasty Bush antiterrorism protocols. But our "to be or not to be" Hamlet also wanted to continue keeping the country safe from another 9/11-style terrorist attack, so he kept Guantanamo open, quadrupled the number of Predator drone attacks, and either preserved or expanded all the Bush protocols that he had once derided.

Abroad, a new multilateral Obama wished to act only in concert with the United Nations and our allies. He vowed to respect the sovereignty of other countries and not meddle in their affairs by imposing American values. And yet, the president also embraced eternal and universal human rights and wanted the United States to be on the correct side of history. So he criticized our intervention to foster democracy in Iraq even as his vice president praised it. We surged in Afghanistan even as we posted deadlines to leave. We promised not to meddle by not supporting Iranian protestors, and then meddled in support of Egyptian protestors.

Hosni Mubarak was a dictator and was not a dictator, who had to leave yesterday, today or maybe tomorrow. The situation in Libya is deemed unacceptable, but how exactly it could be made acceptable has never been spelled out. Intervening there to support rebels is said to be good; but apparently so is supporting Saudi troops intervening in Bahrain to put down rebels and protect the status quo.

Middle East strongmen, the president tells us, are cruel and must leave, but the why and how of it all are also never stated. Are they supposed to flee only when protests reach a critical mass, in Egypt and Tunisia, but not in Saudi Arabia, Syria or Iran?

President Obama has spent most of his life either in, or teaching school...and making laws that he was not responsible for enforcing. His hope-and-change speeches were as moving in spirit as they were lacking in details.

But now Obama is chief executive and learning, as did Prince Hamlet...that thinking out every possible side of a question can mean never acting on any of them. Sort of a Shakespearean prison where "there is nothing either good or bad." Worrying about pleasing everyone ensures pleasing no one. Once again, such conscious does make cowards of us all.

Hamlets, past and present, are as admirable in theory as they are fickle, and in fact...are often dangerous.

Watch what he does, not what he says...The Emperor has no clothes.

CHAPTER 17

How 'bout those Navy Seals...and their complicit collaborators taking out Osama after waiting many, many months for "Hamlet Obama" to grant "permission" for their near perfectly executed mission. And even then, it would appear the go-a-head came only after continuing insistence from various high-level military and CIA officials.

But after hearing his briefing to the public and news media, his mindless supporters must have been thinking, "Oh my gosh, Obama did it all by himself."

Here are a few excerpts from President Obama's speech on Sunday night about the killing of Osama bin Laden.

"Tonight, I can report...And so shortly after taking office, I directed Leon Panetta...I was briefed on a possible lead to bin Laden...I met repeatedly with my national security team...I determined that we had enough intelligence to take action...Today, at my direction...Over the years, I've repeatedly made clear...Tonight, I called President Zardari...My team has also spoken...These efforts weigh on me every time I, as Commander-in-Chief...Finally, let me say to those families...I know that it has, at times, unraveled."

Most of these first-person pronouns could have been replaced by either the first-person plural (our, we) or proper nouns (the United States, America). But they reflect a now well-known Obama trait of personalizing the presidency.

The problem with first-person personalizing national security is twofold. One, it is not consistent. Obama reports good news in terms of "I," bad news is delivered as "reset," "the previous administration," "in the past." All good things abroad are due to Obama himself; all bad things are still the fallout from George W. Bush.

Two, there is the small matter of hypocrisy. The protocols for taking out Osama bin Laden were all established by President Bush and all opposed by Senator and then candidate Obama. Yet President Obama never seeks to explain that disconnect; indeed, he emphasizes it by the overuse of the first person. When the president reminds us this week of what "over the years I've repeatedly made clear," does he include his opposition to what he now has institutionalized?

Guantanamo had proven to be important for gathering intelligence, but candidate Barack Obama derided it as "a tremendous recruiting tool for al-Qaeda."

Some key intelligence was found by interrogating prisoners abroad, but Obama wished to end that practice: "This means ending the practices of shipping prisoners away in the dead of night to be tortured in far-off countries, of detaining thousands without charge or trial, of maintaining a network of secret prisons to jail people beyond the reach of law. That will be my position as president. That includes renditions." Renditions have not ended under Obama, but expanded.

In some cases we are trying suspects through military tribunals and here again, Obama used to deplore the practice he has now adopted. A flawed military-commission system that has failed to convict anyone of a terrorist act since the 9/11 attacks and that has been embroiled in continuing legal challenges.

Senator Obama complained about airborne attacks on the Afghanistan-Pakistan borderlands. President Obama increased Predator assassination attacks fivefold. He has killed four times as many terrorist suspects by Predators in 27 months than did President Bush in eight years.

In January 2007, three weeks after President Bush announced the surge...Senator Obama introduced the "Iraq War De-escalation Act of 2007." If it had passed, that law would have removed all troops from Iraq by March 2008. Obama derided the surge in unequivocal terms both before and after its implementation. "I don't know any expert on the region or any military officer that I've spoken to privately that believes the surge is going to make a substantial difference on the ground situation. Here's what we know...the surge has not worked."

Candidate Obama criticized warrantless wiretaps, in accusing the Bush administration in the harshest terms: "This administration acts like violating civil liberties is the way to enhance our security. It is not." A disinterested examination of present policy regarding both wiretaps and intercepts would show no change from the Bush administration, or indeed considerable expansion of the use of these tools.

If one wonders why former President Bush did not attend ceremonies with President Obama this week in New York, it might be because of past rhetoric like this about policies Obama once derided and then codified: "I taught constitutional law for ten years at the University of Chicago, so...um...your next president will actually believe in the Constitution, which you can't say about your current president. George Bush did not believe in the U.S. Constitution." This from the man who is currently not only walking on the Constitution, he's trampling it.

In sum, Senator Obama opposed tribunals, renditions, Guantanamo, preventive detention, Predator-drone attacks, the Iraq War, wiretaps, and intercepts...before President Obama either continued or expanded nearly all of them, in addition to embracing targeted assassinations, new body scanning and pat-downs at airports, and a third preemptive war against an oil-exporting Arab Muslim nation, this one including NATO efforts to kill the Qaddafi family. The only thing more surreal than Obama's radical transformation is the sudden approval of it by the once hysterical "Left." In Animal Farm and 1984 fashion, the world we knew in 2006 has simply been airbrushed away.

Times change. People say one thing when they are candidates for public office, quite another as officeholders with responsibility of governance. Obama as president naturally does not wish to be treated in the manner in which he once treated President Bush. Conservatives might resent Obama's prior demagoguery at a critical period in our national security, as much as they are relieved that he seems to have grown up and repudiated it.

Okay, the public perhaps understands all that hypocrisy as the stuff of presidential politics. But I think it will not quite accept the next step of taking full credit in hyperbolic first-person fashion for operations that would have been impossible had his views prevailed.

Now that Osama bin Laden is dead, Obama and his liberal-progressives can turn their attention to another remorseless enemy, who for years has sown death and destruction among blameless innocents. I'm referring, of course, to Ronald McDonald.

The McDonald's mascot may qualify as one of the more annoying characters on the planet. But to his credit, he doesn't compound his unappealing personality by bossing you around. In that respect, he is far less objectionable than the people who make a fetish of finding him objectionable.

Last week, they took out ads in several newspapers blaming the clown for childhood obesity and demanding that McDonald's "stop marketing junk food to kids." The signers range from the Physicians Committee for Responsible Medicine, an anti-meat group that the American Medical Association has accused of "perverting medical science," to alternative-healing huckster Andrew Weil.

The general rule of critics is that McDonald's can do nothing right. Some years ago, they insisted that the company get rid of the beef tallow in which it cooked french-fries. It did so, in favor of a supposedly healthier oil containing trans fats. A few years later, the activists demanded that it abandon trans fats, which it soon did.

How much credit did it get for those changes? Not much. The class of people who detested McDonald's...went right on detesting.

These ads are part of a larger campaign against everything McDonald's represents. If the company retired Ronald McDonald, its enemies would just step up their demands for an end to Happy Meals. Get rid of Happy Meals, and they would demand that McDonald's thoroughly revamp its menu to incorporate their superior notions of nutrition.

Ultimately, the only way to please the critics is to become

something unrecognizable. Or, better yet, disappear from the planet. New York Times food columnist Mark Bittman, who is to sanctimony what Saudi Arabia is to oil, believes "anything that discourages people from eating at McDonald's could be seen as wonderful."

Wonderful, that is, to enlightened souls who avoid it at all costs. But it's clear that McDonald's comes much closer to what paying consumers actually want than what its detractors prefer. It has 32,000 restaurants; serving 64 million people a day. Last year, it had revenues of $24 billion, more than the gross domestic product of some countries.

The food moralists imagine that McDonald's marketing magic renders its targets helpless to resist. Ronald McDonald might as well be rounding up kids at gunpoint and forcing them to choke down burgers and fries.

But children young enough to be seduced by Ronald McDonald or Happy Meals rarely visit restaurants without parents. These adults are free agents who should be experienced at saying "no" to protect the interests of their sometimes-ungrateful offspring.

Parents who dislike McDonald's sales tactics have a wealth of dining alternatives. And anyone who wants a low-fat, low-calorie meal can easily find it underneath the Golden Arches: Health magazine ranks McDonald's among the 10 healthiest fast-food restaurants.

It may be argued that many parents are too weak or ignorant to make sound decisions about the food their kids eat. If so, McDonald's and its unstoppable brainwashing machine could vanish tomorrow without making the slightest difference in obesity or other diet-related ailments.

Some people (Mc Donald's critics) don't like cheap, tasty, high-calorie fare because McDonald's offers it. McDonald's offers it because "a lot of people like it." In McDonald's absence, patrons would seek it out at other fast-food places, sit-down establishments or grocery stores.

We live in an age of inexpensive, abundant food carefully designed to please the mass palate. Most of us, recalling the scarcity, monotony and starvation that afflicted our ancestors for a hundred millenniums, count that as progress. But those determined to save human beings from their own alleged folly see it as catastrophic.

What is apparent is that the militant enemies of fast food would like it treated as a public health menace along the lines of tobacco. They want broad measures to restrict, discourage and punish the companies that sell it.

Ronald McDonald is merely a convenient symbol. Their true target is a capitalist economy that gives companies far too much latitude in appealing to customers and allows government far too little control over our food choices.

The idea of using government power to dictate what we eat will strike many Americans as a gross intrusion on personal freedom. But McDonald's enemies...they're lovin' it.

Should parents of extremely obese children lose custody for not controlling their kid's weight? A commentary in one of the nation's most distinguished medical journals argues yes.

It has happened a few times in the U.S., and the opinion piece in today's Journal of the American Medical Association says putting children temporarily in foster care is in some cases more ethical than obesity surgery.

135

Dr. David Ludwig, an obesity specialist at Harvard-affiliated Children's Hospital Boston, said the point isn't to blame parents (of course not), but rather to act in the children's best interest and get them the help that for whatever reason their parents can't (don't) provide.

State intervention "ideally will support not just the child but the whole family, with the goal of reuniting child and family as soon as possible. That may require instructions on parenting (duh)," said Ludwig.

University of Pennsylvania bioethicist, Art Caplan said he worries that the debate risks putting too much blame on parents. Obese children are victims (the victim mentality again) of advertising, marketing, peer pressure and bullying, things a parent can't control.

Where was I going with this McDonald thing, you ask. I'm continuing with my condemnation of irresponsible and/or immature parents; they need to take personal responsibility for their overweight children! The government already has its hands in every aspect of our life because with each passing generation, we're demonstrating that too many...no longer have a clue. I've beat this old school logic to death in the course of writing five books, but our problems today stem from the loss of many of life's guiding principles..."intangibles" that existed in "another time...another place."

Examples: Responsible, accountability, common courtesies, common sense, strong work ethic, loyalty, respect for others and their property, family values, patriotism and love of God and country. The list goes on, but it's history.

CHAPTER 18

Thank goodness I came from a much earlier...and different generation. We worked hard, paid our own way and were patriotic. We've seen our country, our culture, morals, marriage and attitudes change in ways we find very discouraging and hard to believe today. Capitalism served us well as a developing nation. Business, production of durable goods, advancements in technology and the innovative nature of Americans kept America on the cutting edge of modern progress. The United States was the envy of the world.

Our country, having lost its moral-compass, elected an unknown to be our president based on his oratory skills... with a teleprompter. He then wasted no time heading off to Europe and the Middle East to apologize for America's actions over the past 80-plus-years. Once there he proceeded to bow and kiss hands (asses) while decrying and condemning all the "bad things," he felt America was responsible and accountable for. But he neglected to make reference to all the cemeteries filled with young American men and women who gave their lives so that Europe could remain free. Enough said, you got what you voted for...

Is America's preeminent world role over?

That's what a recent New Yorker essay, based on interviews with presidential advisers, claimed. It character-
ized the new Obama foreign-relations style as "leading
from behind"...given the supposedly inevitable American
decline and growing unpopularity. The president is said
to agree with pundits such as Fareed Zakaria and Tom
Friedman, who have often outlined the parameters of
what the post-American world would look like.

But if America abrogates its preeminent leadership position of the last 65 years, wouldn't the world look a lot
like it did in the pre-American days of the 1930s? Then,
a Depression-era United States was just one of many
powers reluctant to assert leadership abroad.

Eighty years ago, a newly Westernized and anti-demo-
cratic Japanese powerhouse, in the fashion of today's
rising China, was carving out uncontested Asian spheres
of influence. An oil, rubber, and iron-hungry imperial
Japan claimed it needed more natural resources to fuel
its industrial revolution, and so spread an authoritarian
Asian co-prosperity sphere of influence as an alternative to an alliance with an economically depressed and
psychologically withdrawn America.

At the time, most Americans were tired of our overseas
commitments. Our ancestors felt that their considerable
sacrifices in World War I had either gone unappreciated
or had solved little, not unlike the way we are becoming
exhausted by Afghanistan, Iraq and now Libya today.

A newly confident, united and ascendant Germany was
growing angry at other European countries. It nursed
a long list of financial grievances over feeling used and
abused. Sound familiar? A weak Britain and France had
almost no confidence in their own declining militaries...

sort of like the sad spectacle of their impotence in Libya that we have witnessed over the last two months.

Much-vaunted international institutions, like the bank-rupt League of Nations, were about as effective in the role of world watchdogs as the corrupt United Nations is today. Europe and America were emerging from the nightmare of financial insolvency.

In the 1930s, the so-called international community cared as much about challenging rising, aggressive to-talitarian countries such as Germany, Italy, Japan and Russia as it does today about ascendant China or Iran. Millions of Jews, then as now, heard crazy threats of their annihilation, and desperately...in vain, looked to the protection of the United States.

In other words, the post-American world could look a lot like the rather terrifying pre-American version of seven decades past. Why in the world would we wish to return to it?

The "declinists" insist we have no choice. Globalization has spread power. America has depleted its resources, both natural and financial. And our prior leadership abroad is something worthy of apology rather than pride anyway. Think of the receding postcolonial Britain around 1946 as our model, not the confident, rising postwar United States of Harry Truman and Dwight D. Eisenhower.

But decline is always a choice, not an inevitable fate. America's known fossil fuel reserves...natural gas, oil, coal, shale, tar-sands, are larger than ever. The problem is not finding more energy but marshaling the will to use the vast new sources of energy we have recently discovered.

Our military is not just larger than the alternatives, but vastly larger and ever more lethal. Given the enormous size and productivity of the U.S. economy, we have the means, but not yet the will...to rapidly pay down our huge debt. In a world short on food, America is the world's greatest agricultural producer.

Other industrialized populations aged and declined; ours is still growing. America is widely criticized abroad even as it remains by far the favored destination of global immigrants. Diverse religious practice is still vibrant in the United States. Elsewhere, it is fossilized in Europe, nonexistent in China, and intolerant in the Middle East.

While riots, strikes or revolutions sweep southern Europe and the Middle East, the United States remains stable and quiet...despite far greater racial, ethnic and religious diversity. Globalization is still mostly a phenomenon of American innovation and originality to be licensed and outsourced abroad.

There have been plenty of thugs who threatened their neighbors over the last 30 years. Saddam Hussein, Slobodan Milosevic, Manuel Noriega and the Taliban were all deposed from rule by American power only. The "lost" war in Iraq resulted in a democratic and, for now, still viable government in place of genocide. Afghanistan is depressing, but the medieval Taliban has remained out of power for nearly a decade.

In short, the old pre-American world was as unstable and dangerous as would be a new post-American update. But both retrenchments were choices that an unsure and depressed United States made...not symptoms, then or now, of inherent weakness or inevitable decline.

CHAPTER 19

Vulnerability of a Disarmed Citizenry:

As you may have surmised, I'm not concerned so much about crime as I am about the vulnerability of a disarmed citizenry from tyranny by their own government. You may think that is a reckless statement about crime, but it isn't. I base it on evidence that indicates to me that crime is not our greatest danger. In my humble opinion, crime is manageable through law enforcement.

The pro-gun counter-argument claims that the U.S. has a murder rate 5 times higher than the "unfree" countries that do not allow private handgun ownership. This is untrue. Perhaps they're referring to the total number of murders...or spinning the truth. The total may be higher in some unfree countries, but so is the population. There are many unfree countries with much higher rates per capita than the U.S.; Russia and South Africa come to mind, for instance. And the rate isn't higher just in those miserable places.

But old impressions die hard: Americans still think of Britain as a low-crime country. Conversely, the British still think of America as a high-crime country. Neither impression is true. For instance, in America about 12 percent of all burglaries are "Hot" (while the owners are present), while in Britain it is over half. Americans would be outraged if such statistics existed in the U.S. And while the odds are higher that you can be shot to death here in America, in Britain you are more likely to be strangled to death.

Take your pick.

As for misperceptions about guns, one may ask why people believe that guns in the hands of law-abiding citizens are so dangerous? It is because they are inundated by a liberal media with stories of children being killed by guns. The media have a saying: "If it bleeds, it leads"... meaning it becomes the lead story.

Our disgraceful president, an ardent advocate of gun control, loves to say that 12 "kids" die each day from gun violence. What he doesn't mention is that 80 percent of those kids are between the ages of 15 and 19, nearly all of whom are involved in gangs, convenience-store hold-ups, and drug deals, etc. When confronted with that statistic, the socialists immediately leap to the argument that so many young children die from guns found in the home that errant fathers leave lying around. So lets look at that: Taking a typical year, say 1996, there were a total of 1,134 accidental firearm deaths in the entire United States. Of that number, 42 were under the age of ten. That's less than one per state. In comparison, during the same period the same age group suffered 2,404 motor-vehicle deaths, 805 lost their lives drowning, and fire and burns killed 738. Source: National Center for Injury Prevention, Injury Mortality Statistics, Atlanta: Centers for Disease Control, 1999.

Almost twice as many children drown in their own bath-tubs each year than die from all types of firearm accidents. Or how about the study which found that child-resistant bottle caps have resulted in 3,500 additional poisonings annually of children under the age of 5 from aspirin-related drugs because people have been lulled into a less-safety-conscious mode of behavior by the existence of safety caps. What does that say for the hue-and-cry for safety locks on guns? Not that I'm personally opposed to them in households with kids, I'm just asking. The point is, 42 kids are accidentally killed with guns, which is terrible, but a hundred times that number are accidentally killed by vehicles, drowning and fire, and an additional 3,500 are poisoned by just one common legal product...and what gets on the news?

Those guns again!

If one is so fervent about the dangers of guns, they should be positively astonished at learning how few people, out of nearly 300-million in the United states, actually die by guns each year. Mathematically, the number looks something like this: 0.00012.

So the real question should be, are more lives lost or saved by law-abiding citizens having guns? The answer is unequivocal; more guns in the hands of law-abiding citizens results in less crime. The largest study ever conducted on this question found, overwhelming and conclusive evidence, that more guns equal less crime. Source: Dr. John R. Lott, Jr., "More Guns, Less Crime: Understanding Crime and Gun Control Laws," University of Chicago Press, 1997. Dr. Lott is a senior research scholar in the School of Law at Yale University...hardly a bastion of Conservatism.

As I said in the beginning, my primary concern is not with crime, it is with tyranny in government. When I look at recent history, I see tens-of-millions murdered by their own governments, and in each case, the government first disarmed them, thereby taking away their ability to resist. When I weigh that against the few who die each year by guns (unfortunate as that is), I immediately conclude that it is much safer for a law-abiding society to be armed. And that doesn't even place on the scales when compared with the benefits of less crime perpetrated upon an armed society. You might say that there are places in the world where there is stability despite a shortage of guns. You might also say that you see the U.S. foreign policy as patchy, though well intentioned. I don't know if the two are related, but I would question how stable anywhere in the world would be if Americans hadn't defended freedom around the globe with the notable exception of the lunatic foreign policy of the present U.S. Administration, which blithely "Wags The Dog."

I think I have a fair impression of various societies around the world and I would wager that as long as America remains a strong and free nation, the rest of the industrialized world, on the whole, can safely practice internal gun-control without consequence to their sovereignty. But God have mercy on them if America should ever fall, because there will be no one to come to their aid. Some say that China will be the premiere world power within this century. How does the prospect of China defending your liberty strike you? And people shouldn't lull themselves into thinking that it couldn't happen to America. All nations eventually decay and disintegrate. That's History 101. The unknown is: When?

The one thing that would most certainly hasten it, in America, is gun control, and most heavy-duty thinkers on the subject are of the opinion that the liberal socialist gun-abolishionists, with the help of a sympathetic liberal press, are winning the PR game. We know that Constitutions are not immutable. That is correct (if you remember); we changed ours about 70 years ago abolishing booze, and then changed it back again. It is entirely possible that the socialists will win, and get our Second Amendment repealed. I don't think it will happen, but it is possible. All I can say is: God help us if they do. I don't think that if they are successful we will be able to reverse it before it is too late.

The bottom line is, whether we are talking about crime or about liberty, forbidding law-abiding people to have guns is an absolute folly. We must always remember that it's never about the guns; it is...first and foremost, about "control."

Most commonly, an aspiring dictator disarms the population, thereby facilitating an easy slaughter of the opposition. As a population, it is expedient for us to understand both historical and modern examples of how dictators have used civilian disarmament to attain and maintain absolute control, that we might recognize instances and/or evident in our society and immediately curtail such efforts.

Dictatorships, both past and present, follow common patterns. While their methods for attaining their powerful positions may vary: Adolf Hitler and Hugo Chavez were freely elected, Joseph Stalin slowly developed his prominence within the ruling political party, and Mao Tse-Tung and Fidel Castro led violent revolutions; they then facilitated their increasing stronghold on the population through similar measures.

During the ascension to power, most dictators gain popular support by exploiting the fears and desires of the people. The way Hitler gained control of Germany serves as an illustration of the pattern all prominent 20th century dictators used to secure absolute control. In the aftermath of World War I, Germany was left in ruins and was forced to bear the full blame and cost the war had wrought. The result was a nation where unemployment, food shortages and economic hardship were rampant. The German people were forced to finance reconstruction efforts, leaving them economically crippled. To add insult to injury, Germans were not allowed a voice on the international stage in directing those reconstructive efforts, leaving them socially crippled. It was this climate of victimization that made fertile the soil in which Hitler would grow into power.

While writing a recent documentary on how Hitler was able to rise to power, National Review editor Dave Kopel, and Psychologist Richard Griffiths, who specialize in researching gun issues, scrutinized that if we are serious about "never again," then we must be serious about remembering how and why Hitler was able to accomplish what he did. Hitler began his rise to power by promising to redeem Germany, making her once again, a great power, compelling her to be esteemed in international circles, and by enacting dramatic social purifications that would create a more perfect society.

Political desires to improve one's nation are not uncommon, nor undesirable. The distinct difference between an honest politician and a would-be dictator will become transparent only after they take power. What's that old saying, "Talk is cheap."

Because the policies of Nazi Germany were carried and imposed upon every nation in occupied Europe, coupled with the direct aggression propagated by the Nazis, there is an abundance of information on Hitler's policies to disarm civilian populations, thus examples from Nazi Germany are many, but the same patterns were followed by the other aforementioned dictators. Dr. Miguel Faria Jr., who escaped Cuba as a political refugee, after Castro seized control, describes the universal nature of this pattern:

Frequently, when presented with these deadly chronicles (of the many dictatorships that disarmed their civilians) and the perilous historic sequence...namely, that gun registration is followed by banning, confiscation, civilian disarmament and ultimately, by authoritarianism; naïve Americans lecture that it cannot happen here!

Germany's prelude to significant disarmament began during the Weimar Republic, when expansive registration and record keeping requirements of firearms and firearm owners were mandated in 1929. On these policies Dave Kopel and Richard Griffiths write:

"Under the Weimar law, no license was needed to possess a firearm in the home unless the citizen owned more than five guns of a particular type or stored more than 100 cartridges. The law's requirements were more relaxed for firearms of a hunting or sporting type. Indeed, the Weimar statute was the world's first gun law to create formal distinction between sporting and non-sporting firearms. Significantly, the Weimar law required the registration of most lawfully owned firearms. In Germany, the Weimar registration program law provided the information which the Nazis needed to disarm the Jews and others considered untrustworthy."

In 1938, after Hitler had taken power, he expanded the registration requirements and began to compile the data on firearm owners as well as the types and quantities of the firearms possessed. The original purpose of the Weimar registration requirements was to provide for public safety by controlling who could possess firearms and to allow the government to regulate their use. Antithetically, passive registration in the name of public safety gave Hitler the ability to begin complete disarmament.

In order to gain proper perspective on firearms and public safety, the modern American saga on this issue serves as a dynamic vehicle. Those in the United States who support the registration and restriction of firearms possession among civilians, the foremost of which is the Brady Campaign to Prevent Gun Violence, lay public safety as the primary reason for such restrictions. The quote below is from the Brady Campaign to Prevent Gun Violence website:

"In order to stem the flow of handgun violence, America needs a national system of handgun owner licensing. Handguns should be treated like cars in that owners would be licensed and handguns would be registered. Congress would establish minimum standards for the licensing system, which would be implemented by the states. Licensing and registration will also provide law enforcement with the means to prevent individuals like... (here a list of several murderers is inserted) from obtaining guns (2007)."

The Brady Campaign website provides for similar restrictions on all other types of firearms as well, making distinctions between sporting and non-sporting firearms. Although it seems logical, one is still left to ask if gun registration and other restrictions really do serve the public safety and if they do in fact reduce crime.

According to statistics posted on the Brady Campaign homepage (2007): In 2004, there were 11,344 firearm related murders in the United States. This is a significant number of deaths, but when removed from isolation, it shrinks in its shock value. There are approximately 193 million legally owned firearms in about 80 million U.S. households (Kleck, Gertz, 1998), making each individual firearm statistically unlikely to be used in a murder. Furthermore, according to research conducted by University of Florida Professors and Criminologists Gary Kleck and Marc Gertz, (1998), privately owned firearms are used between 1.2 million and 2.2 million times per year to prevent crime in the United States, significantly outweighing the perceived costs of private firearms ownership. Further logical deductions can be made regarding the true dispositions of using gun control as a crime deterrent. First and foremost, criminals, or people who break the law, don't care if a gun is outlawed. Thus, even when guns are completely banned, criminals are still armed. Secondly, registration information is used by law enforcement to investigate crimes, and has rarely, if ever, been used to prevent crime. Thirdly, law enforcement is rarely able to prevent violent crime, but typically arrive after the criminal has left the scene. In the United States, the most significant reductions in violent crime have occurred in the states that have removed restrictions on civilian's right to carry a handgun (Kleck, Gertz, 1998). Thus, public safety is not at all strengthened by the registration and restriction of firearms; in fact it is significantly weakened.

Firearm registration and restriction has seldom started after a dictator has gained absolute power, rather, the dictator exploited already existing laws. On November 9th, 1938, Nazi SS troops, armed with the lists of registered gun owners created under the Weimar government, raided Jewish homes enforcing a newly signed decree by Hitler: "Ordering all Jews to be disarmed. In the event of resistance, they are to be shot immediately." Once the confiscation was complete, on the 10th of November 1938, Nazis began to loot, burn, and destroy Jewish property, forcing the Jews either into ghettos or concentration camps. With no resistance, the operation was completed quickly. The Jews who were relocated in the ghettos were subjected to ever increasing restrictions on the possession on weapons. Dr. Stephen P. Halbrook Ph. D, J.D. described this condition:

"All hell broke loose on November 10; Nazis smashed, looted and burned Jewish shops and temples. One of the first legal measures issued was an order by Heinrich Himmler, commander of all German police, forbidding Jews to possess any weapons whatever and imposing a penalty of twenty years confinement in a concentration camp upon every Jew found in possession of a weapon hereafter. Thousands of Jews were taken away. Searches of Jewish homes were calculated to seize firearms and assets and to arrest adult males."

The Nazi raids on Jewish homes in Germany continued to intensify as WWII spread across Europe. In each country, the Nazis occupied, one of the first orders of business was to post a notice ordering the occupied citizens to surrender their firearms on penalty of death.

Although the Nazis faced armed resistance in every country they occupied until the end of the war, the fact that other European countries also had laws requiring police records to be kept on persons who possessed firearms, it was a simple matter to identify gun owners. Many of them disappeared in the middle of the night along with political opponents. As the Nazis exploited firearm registration and licensing requirements, most opposition groups were severely crippled, facilitating the rapid spread of Nazism.

While the Nazis made good on the threat to execute persons in possession of firearms, the gun control decree was not entirely successful. Partisans launched armed attacks. But resistance was hampered by the lack of civilian arms possession.

In 1943, there was one such uprising in the Warsaw, Poland ghetto. Here several Jewish men, despite being woefully outnumbered, and armed with only a few old handguns, began to fight the Nazis. With the conviction to protect their lives and their families, this small band of armed men were able to fend off the Nazi forces for several days. Dr. Halbrook describes this act of astonishing bravery:

"Out of all the acts of armed citizen resistance in the war, the Warsaw Ghetto Uprising of 1943 is difficult to surpass in its heroism. Beginning with just a few handguns, armed Jews put a temporary stop to the deportation and extermination camps, frightened the Nazis out of the ghetto, stood off assaults for days on end, and escaped to the forests to continue the struggle."

Even though this particular uprising failed to permanently expel the Nazis, Dr. Halbrook asks: "What if there had been two, three, many Warsaw ghetto uprisings?" If not for the forceful disarming of the citizens, it is unlikely the Nazis could have been nearly as successful. Those Jewish men demonstrated that a lot of courage and a little weaponry could do much to stem the prevailing tide of a monstrous dictatorship. But the failure of these courageous men demonstrated that the use of civilian disarmament was a very significant factor in facilitating Hitler's murder of about 21 million people, excluding war casualties.

Unbeknownst to many Americans, who having seen and experienced mostly the goodness of America, gun registration is the gateway to civilian disarmament, which often precedes genocide. In the monumental book "Lethal Laws," published by Jews for the Preservation of Firearm Ownership, we learn that authoritarian governments that conducted genocide and mass killings of their own populations first disarmed their citizens. The recipe for accomplishing this goal went as follows...demonizing guns, registration, then banning and confiscation, and finally total civilian disarmament.

Enslavement of the people then followed with limited resistance, as was the case in Nazi Germany, the Soviet

Union, Red China, Cuba and other totalitarian regimes of the 20th century.

By virtue of the fact that this identical pattern of civilian disarmament is found at the root of virtually every mass killing in the 20th century, modern governments should be very careful when contemplating firearm registration and restriction requirements. The importance of gun control measures, to the dictators themselves, is revealed in the writings of Mao Tse-Tung, when he wrote:

"Firearms are the most important of all weapons, and it should be guaranteed that they are in the 'hands of the armed forces' of the workers and peasants. Undertaking an investigation and banning privately owned firearms, and carrying out the registration of firearms constitute important tasks in ensuring the victory of the revolution."

As the "most important of all weapons," the possession of firearms is in reality the possession of power. Dictators cannot subdue an armed population, and an unarmed population cannot overthrow a dictator.

Modern efforts to require the registration and restriction of civilian firearms come from many fronts, from organizations like America's Brady Campaign to the United Nations. Even though we may not perceive a direct threat of impending dictatorship, the pattern of how they begin is well in motion. And perhaps the most effective reminder to any aspiring dictator is that armed citizens are capable and willing to fight for a democracy any dictator is seeking to usurp.

During the past year, Venezuelan president, Hugo Chavez, has declared that he is "temporarily" taking complete control in order to quickly move his country toward a more independent and more prominent world position.

He has already taken control of all Venezuelan oil and utilities, and has made moves to decrease the voice of his opponents by restricting political representation to those who agree with him. Venezuela already had mandatory firearm registration and many restrictions, and although Chavez had yet to take any overt action against those who do possess firearms, he certainly has all the tools he would need to do so. In the space of only a few months, Chavez has gone from a freely elected democratic President, to a socialist autocrat.

Illustrating the use of an armed population to protect a nation from dictatorship, James Madison, (1787), one of America's Founding Fathers, said in the Federalist Papers:

"Besides the advantages of being armed, which the Americans possess over the people of almost every other nation, the existence of subordinate governments, to which the people are attached and by which the militia officers are appointed, forms a barrier against the enterprises of ambition, more insurmountable than any which a simple government of any form can admit of."

It was well understood by America's Founding Fathers that the only way a nation can remain forever free from the tyranny of dictatorship is to maintain an armed population. History shows that the cost of disarming civilians is very high. Conservative estimates put the number of unarmed civilians killed by their own governments at over 56 million people in the past century.

History has given us many examples to clearly show the pattern dictators use to seize and maintain control. Modern politics in both domestic and international arenas are beginning to show a widespread increase in the prevalence of the dictatorship pattern and civilian disarmament. If the populations of the world are to resist dictatorship and if we truly desire to "never again" allow monsters like Hitler, Stalin, and Mao to seize power, our most basic protection is the ability to counter with armed resistance. The people of the world must never be disarmed; we all need to recognize this insidious way that a nation can rapidly slip from freedom to tyranny. As a means of self preservation, and to preserve our freedom, we should all be armed, trained, and vigilant in killing the seeds of tyranny that are being sown by those who would disarm us.

The natural tendency of every government is to grow steadily worse...that is, to grow more satisfactory to those who constitute it and less satisfactory to those who are expected to support it.

"I know no class of my fellowmen, however just, enlightened, and humane, which can be wisely and safely trusted absolutely with the liberties of any other class."

Frederick Douglass

CHAPTER 19: PART 2

The Brownshirts:

An early Nazi paramilitary organization, the Sturm Abteilung or SA (assault division), was assembled under the pseudonym, the "Brownshirts." The Brownshirts were recruited from various rough elements of society and was the brainchild of Adolt Hitler in 1921.

Fitted out in brown uniforms reminiscent of Mussolini's Blackshirts, they figured prominently in organized marches and rallies. Their violent intimidation of political opponents and of Jews played a key role in Hitler's rise to power. But by the time 1931 rolled around, a radical anti-capitalist, Ernst Röhm, was leading the SA. By 1933 it numbered some two million, double the size of Germany's army, which was hostile to them. Röhm's ambition was that the SA should achieve parity with the army and the Nazi Party, and serve as the vehicle for a Nazi revolution in state and society.

For Hitler, the main consideration was to ensure the loyalty to his regime of the German establishment, and in particular of the German officer corps. Consequently, he had more than 70 members of the SA, including Röhm, summarily executed (June 29, 1934) by the SchutzStaffel or SS (Stormtroopers) during the "Night of the Long Knives." From that point on, the SA was, for all practical intents and purposes, effectively superseded by the SS, though never formally dissolved.

Fast forward, March 24, 2009:

Obama's "Brownshirts" bill is working its way through the Senate.

This dangerous bill is unquestionably nothing less than a way to further fund and indoctrinate more foot soldiers for the Democratic Party, following the Marxist model of Saul Alinsky.

Barack Obama was a founding member of the board of Public Allies in 1992, resigning before his wife became executive director of the Chicago chapter of Public Allies in 1993. Obama plans to use the nonprofit group, which he features on his campaign Website, as the model for a national service corps. He calls his Orwellian program, "Universal Voluntary Public Service."

Big Brother has nothing on the Obamas. They plan to herd American youth into government-funded re-education camps where they'll be brainwashed into thinking America is a racist, oppressive place in need of "social change."

The pitch that Public Allies makes on its Website doesn't seem all that radical. It promises to place young adults (18-30) in paid one-year "community leadership" positions with nonprofit or government agencies. They'll also be required to attend weekly training workshops and three retreats.

In exchange, they'll get a monthly stipend of up to $1,800, plus paid healthcare and childcare. They also get a post-service education award of $4,725 that can be used to pay off past student loans or fund future education.

But its real mission is to radicalize America's youth and use them to bring about "social change" through threats, pressure, tension and confrontation...the tactics used by the father of community organizing, Saul "The Red" Alinsky.

The legislation also refers to "uniforms" that would be worn by the "volunteers" and the "need for a public service academy, a 4-year institution to focus on training future public sector leaders." The training, apparently, would occur at "campuses."

The vote on H.R. 1388 came yesterday, which re-authorized, through 2014, the National and Community Service Act of 1990 and the Domestic Volunteer Service Act of 1973, acts that originally, among other programs, funded the AmeriCorps and the National Senior Service Corps.

It not only re-authorized the programs, but also includes "new programs and studies" and is expected to be funded with an allocation of $6 billion over the next five years, according to the Congressional Budget Office.

Many, however, are raising concerns that the program, which is intended to include 250,000 volunteers, is the beginning of what President Obama called his "National Civilian Security Force" in a speech last year in which he urged creating an organization as big and well-funded as the U.S. military. No one, apparently with the exception of infants, would be excluded.

The new bill specifically references the "possibilities" that all individuals in the United States "could be" expected to perform national service and/or be required to perform a certain amount of national service.

Such new requirements perhaps, the legislation notes, "would strengthen the social fabric of the Nation and overcome civic challenges by bringing together people from diverse economic, ethnic, and educational backgrounds."

This could be the means to develop awareness of national service and volunteer opportunities at a young age by creating, expanding, and promoting service options for elementary and secondary school students, through service learning or other means, and by raising awareness of existing incentives.

According to a report by the Canada Free Press: "The 'Volunteerism' that has kept America running since the days of its founding, would be wiped out with the stroke of a pen. It then becomes forced labor and, like the practice of another era, presses American citizens of all ages and creeds, unknowingly, into military service," the commentary said.

On paper, H.R. 1388 is the "Generations Invigorating Volunteerism and Education Act," but the more innocuous sounding "The Give Act," is the public version...for short, they say.

"The Give Act puts the finishing touches to Public Allies New Leadership for New Times, modeled after Saul Alinsky's Peoples' Organizations and operates under Michelle Obama," the commentary said.

Scary stuff, but it got virtually no coverage in the media. The media would never play that over and over while demanding an explanation. Sarah Palin's pregnant daughter was much more newsworthy, as bad-mouthing material for their liberal constituency.

As a serious student of history, I never thought I would come to experience what the ordinary, moral German must have felt in the mid-1930s. In those times, the "savior" was a former smooth-talking rabble-rouser from the streets, about whom the average German knew next to nothing. What they should have known was that he was associated with groups that shouted, shoved, and pushed people around if they disagreed with them; he edged his way onto the political stage through great oratory.

And there were the promises: Economic times were tough, people were losing jobs, and he was a great speaker. He smiled and frowned and waved a lot. People, and even newspapers, were afraid to speak out for fear that his "brownshirts" would bully and beat them into submission. Which they did, regularly. And then, he was duly elected to office, while a full-throttled economic crisis bloomed at hand...the Great Depression.

Slowly, but surely he seized the controls of government power, person by person, department by department, bureaucracy by bureaucracy. The children of German citizens were at first, encouraged to join a Youth Movement in his name where they were taught exactly what to think. Later, they were required to do so. No Jews of course.

How did he get people on his side? He did it by promising jobs to the jobless, money to the money-less, and rewards for the military-industrial complex. He did it by indoctrinating the children, advocating gun control, health care for all, better wages, better jobs, and promising to re-instill pride, once again, in the country, across Europe and across the world. He did it with a compliant media...did you know that? And he did all this in the name of justice and...change. The people surely got what they voted for.

If you think I am exaggerating, look it up. It's all there in the history books.

Many people of conscience objected in 1933 and were shouted down, called names, laughed at, and ridiculed. When Winston Churchill pointed out the obvious in the late 1930s, while seated in the House of Lords in England (he was not yet Prime Minister), he was booed into his seat and called a crazy troublemaker. He was right, though. And the world came to regret that he was not listened to.

Do not forget that Germany was the most educated, the most cultured country in Europe. It was full of music, art, museums, hospitals, laboratories, and universities. And yet, in less than six years (a shorter time span than just two terms of the United States presidency) it was rounding up its own citizens, killing others, abrogating its laws, turning children against parents and neighbors against neighbors.

As a practical thinker, one not overly prone to emotional decisions, I have choices: I can either believe what the objective pieces of evidence tell me (even if they make me cringe with disgust); I can believe what history is shouting to me from across the chasm of seven decades, or I can hope I am wrong, close my eyes and ignore the proven truism that history repeats itself, have another latte and ignore what is transpiring around me.

CHAPTER 20

O ver a decade ago, one of the greatest leaders in the history of the NRA gave a speech at Harvard Law School entitled: "Winning the Cultural War."

In that speech, Charlton Heston said, "I believe that we are once again engaged in a great civil war, a cultural war that's about to hijack your birthright to think and say what resides within your heart. I fear you can no longer trust the pulsing lifeblood of liberty inside you... the stuff that made this country rise from wildness into the miracle that it is today."

Fighting the culture war was one of Charlton Heston's passions. In that speech, he highlighted the political correctness that was spreading across America, warned of its damaging impact on our First Amendment freedoms, and challenged those students to fight against it.

But the culture war is also being fought against the Second Amendment. In the most basic sense, it is a struggle to define what is "acceptable" in society and, by extension...what is not.

For many years, the anti-gun movement has sought to

make gun ownership socially "unacceptable." They portray gun owners as irresponsible and reckless. They present anyone who believes in owning a gun for self-defense as paranoid. They attack hunters as uneducated rednecks.

Their goal is simple. If they can succeed in reducing the number of gun owners, they will reduce the number of people who are willing to work to protect the fundamental "Right to Keep and Bear Arms."

The progressive liberals are the wedge-drivers in our cultural divide and they are well equipped with a formable array of contrivances. With political correctness muzzling the opposition and our courts (at every level) becoming more and more progressive with their renderings...the handwriting would seem to already be on the wall.

Obama's full court press, against our Constitution, continues with his second appointment to the Supreme Court. Elena Kagan brings with her a globalistic worldview that presents a danger as old as the book of Genesis.

When she was Dean of Harvard Law School, Kagan struck the requirement that her law students study the United States Constitution. Instead, she replaced that course requirement with a new one, the mandatory study of foreign law and international legal standards. In a 2006 press release, Kagan explained that the purpose was to confront law students with the larger universe of legal norms, and to study global networks of law so they could appreciate law from a global sphere rather than strictly from an American constitutional standpoint. During her confirmation hearing to serve as Solicitor General under the Obama Administration, she indicated that as our nation's top government legal advocate, arguing cases before the Supreme Court, she would not hesitate to make arguments based not only on our Constitution, but also on international law as well.

Elena Kagan's loyalty to global law is crucial for two reasons:

First, as a Supreme Court justice, she could be the all-important fifth vote in favor of interpreting our Constitution, not according to the vision of our Founding Fathers, but from an international law standpoint, a concept that would have seemed treasonous to our Founders. Three justices on the Court have already relied on foreign law in their opinions, Justices Kennedy, Breyer and Ginsburg. Recently installed Justice Sotomayor has praised Ruth Bader Ginsberg's penchant for international law, so we can assume she will be a legal globalist as well. Five justices create a majority and with Kagan on board they could begin radically steering us away from the Constitution...that honors our Judeo-Christian heritage and founding.

Second, if this happens...and it's already a given, it will usher America into a new age of global law. With Elena Kagan on the Supreme Court, international legal standards could well be imposed on Americans by the High Court's legal globalists, even without the Senate approving a specific international treaty. In their new novel, "Edge of Apocalypse," Tim LaHaye and Craig Parshall show how this trend might create a modern-day legal nightmare for conscientious Christians. We need only to turn to Genesis, Chapter 11, to see how God opposed the ancient attempt at global unification; the Lord declared the tragic result that would follow if a centralized group of fallen men were to consolidate an unlimited, unrestrained power over the planet.

But an interesting side note to the Kagan appointment and "Obamacare" has surfaced. It's pretty much acknowledged today that the constitutionality of Obamacare will eventually be decided by the Supreme Court...imagine that. And I have no doubt about which way his two newly appointed justices would vote, but currently there is a flickering ray of hope.

It seems there might just be a minor, but annoying conflict of interest here:

The House Judiciary Committee is launching a probe into Supreme Court Justice Elena Kagan's prior involvement with healthcare reform legislation that could determine that she must recuse herself from future high court deliberations on Obamacare.

When President Barack Obama signed the healthcare bill into law, Kagan was still serving as his solicitor general and was responsible for defending the administration's position in federal court cases.

In one series of email exchanges between Kagan and staffers, her top deputy says about legal challengers to Obamacare: "Let's crush them!"

A federal law prohibits a Supreme Court justice from judging a case if while in previous government service he or she served as counsel or adviser on the case or expressed an opinion about its merits, CNS News reported.

A letter sent by 49 members of the House, on June 24, triggered the Judiciary Committee's investigation. It called on the committee "to promptly investigate the extent to which U.S. Supreme Court Justice Elena Kagan was involved in preparing a legal defense of the Patient Protection and Affordable Care Act (PPACA) during her tenure as solicitor general."

Chairman Lamar Smith and Attorney General Eric Holder were both advised of the request.

On June 24, 2011, I (House Judiciary Committee Chairman, Lamar Smith) received the enclosed letter from 49 Members of Congress. On their behalf, I'm writing to request relevant documents and witness interviews in order to properly understand U.S. Supreme Court Associate Justice Elena Kagan's involvement in health care legislation or litigation while serving as United States solicitor general.

In recent weeks, questions have been raised about whether Justice Kagan's prior work on what became the Patient Protection and Affordable Care Act (PPACA), while serving as solicitor general, should disqualify her from hearing challenges to its constitutionality.

All parties agree the critical question is the extent of her involvement, as solicitor general, in formulating the administration's legal position on PPACA, which was signed into law by President Obama on March 23, 2010.

On that day, Virginia and Florida filed suits challenging the constitutionality of the law. President Obama would not nominate Kagan for the Supreme Court until seven weeks later.

The letter from the 49 House members pointed to documents released by the Justice Department in response to a Freedom of Information Act request from CNSNews. com on May 25, 2010.

One item released by the DOJ is an email chain showing that on Jan. 8, 2010, then-Solicitor General Kagan assigned her top deputy, Neal Katyal, to handle the expected lawsuits against Obamacare, and that Katyal informed the Associate Attorney General's office that Kagan "definitely" wanted her office involved in this issue.

Brian Hauck, the senior counsel to Associate Attorney General Tom Perrelli, emailed Katyal to tell him that

Perrelli wanted "to put together a group to get thinking about how to defend against the inevitable challenges to the healthcare proposals that are pending."

Katyal replied: "Absolutely right on. Let's crush them. I'll speak to Solicitor General Elena Kagan and designate someone."

Kagan instantly assigned Katyal.

Chairman Smith's letter to Holder includes a request to interview Katyal.

During Kagan's confirmation hearings in the Senate Judiciary Committee, which began on June 28, 2010, Republicans asked her if she had ever been "asked about her opinion regarding the underlying legal or constitutional issues related to any proposed healthcare legislation...or the underlying legal or constitutional issues related to potential litigation resulting from such legislation." They also asked her whether she had "ever offered any views or comments" on those subjects.

Kagan answered both questions, "No."

On July 20, 2010, the Judiciary Committee voted 13-to-6 to recommend Kagan's confirmation to the full Senate. On August 5, the Senate confirmed her nomination by a vote of 63-to-37. She was sworn in on August 7, 2010.

Chairman Smith gave the Justice Department a July 29 deadline to produce the documents it has requested.

If the court(s) should eventually declare Obamacare constitutional, it will represent one more step toward our voluntary enslavement. A few chapters back I wrote about how government is, and has been for a long time... developing a dependent constituency that will continue voting for them as long as those representatives keep the entitlements coming. We could even describe their relationship as a codependency thing. An arrangement based on indenture, and in this case...it works both ways. "You scratch my back...and I'll scratch your back." In today's world, "what's in it for me" seems to be the driving incentive for our self-indulged populace.

As the government does more and more for the people, the people do less and less for themselves. Over the decades this troubling, self-perpetuating, self-serving arrangement has produced generations of self-indulged Americans. They don't even have to think for themselves anymore, the government does that also...and then tells them how or what to "think" and do.

Kinda like living on Uncle Sam's plantation.

Roll-Call Vote on Justice Brown (June 8, 2005), Janice Rogers Brown, the daughter of an African-American share-cropper from Alabama, who was confirmed Wednesday to the federal appeals court, often invokes slavery in describing what she sees as the perils of liberalism.

Janice Rogers Brown said in one speech that a government without limits on its power has a warrant for oppression.

In the heyday of liberal democracy, all roads lead to slavery, she has warned in speeches. Society and the courts have turned away from the founder's emphasis on personal responsibility, she has argued...and toward a culture of government regulations and dependency that threatens fundamental freedoms.

We no longer find slavery abhorrent, she told the conservative Federalist Society a few years ago. We embrace it. She explained in another speech, if we can invoke no ultimate limits on the power of government, a democracy is inevitably transformed into a "kleptocracy"...a license to steal, a warrant for oppression.

To her critics, such remarks are evidence of extremism. Some Senate Democrats have even singled her out as the most objectionable of President Bush's more than 200 judicial nominees, citing her criticism of affirmative action and abortion rights, but most of all, her sweeping denunciations of New Deal legal precedents that enabled many federal regulations and social programs...developments she has called "the triumph of our socialist revolution."

Her friends and supporters say her views of slavery underpin her judicial philosophy. It was her study of that history, they say, combined with her evangelical Christian faith and her self-propelled rise from poverty that led her to abandon the liberal views she learned from her family.

Her friend and mentor Steve Merksamer, a lawyer in Sacramento, California said, "We have discussed things like, how did slavery and segregation happen?" It comes down to the fact that she believes, as I do, that some things are, in fact, right and some things are, in fact, wrong. Segregation, even though the courts had sustained it for a hundred years...was morally and legally indefensible, and yet it was the law of the land. She brings that philosophy to her legal work.

On the California Supreme Court, her opinions have reflected the philosophy and language of her speeches. In an opinion involving fees charged to San Francisco hotel owners, she proclaimed that private property, already an endangered species in California, is now entirely extinct in San Francisco.

In an affirmative action case, she criticized entitlement programs based on group representation.

Two years after President Bush first nominated her, the Senate voted 56 to 43 to confirm Justice Brown. She was the second of three appellate court nominees who had been blocked by Senate Democrats until a compromise was reached.

Justice Brown, though, was the focus of special attention from both sides in the Senate. For one thing, she was named to the Court of Appeals for the District of Columbia Circuit, widely considered the most influential appellate court and currently almost evenly divided between Republican and Democratic appointees. And even before her confirmation, however, she was often cited as a potential candidate for the Supreme Court, in part because of her politically appealing life story.

She was born Janice Olivia Allen in Greenville, Alabama, in 1949, five years before the Supreme Court struck down segregation in Brown v. Board of Education. After returning from service in World War II, her father grew cotton, corn and peanuts on a 158-acre plot of land he leased, but he eventually re-enlisted. After her parents split up, her grandmother, Beulah Allen became her primary caretaker and raised her until her teenage years, when her mother, a nurse, took her to Sacramento (her mother remarried, adding the name Rogers).

Her family was involved in the voting rights movement in Alabama and became liberal Democrats. She was inspired to become a lawyer by the career of Fred D. Gray, an Alabama civil rights lawyer who represented Martin Luther King Jr. and Rosa Parks. Justice Brown has said she initially shared her family's views, but over the years became more conservative in her thinking.

In California, she made her way through Sacramento State University in part by working at the Department of Corrections, where she met her first husband, Alan

Brown, an administrator there. Soon after the birth of their son, Mr. Brown died of cancer, leaving her to finish college and then law school, at the University of California, Los Angeles, as a single working mother.

After graduating in 1977, she became a legal counsel to the State Legislature and joined the attorney general's office. There she helped successfully defend the state against a class action suit charging that it underpaid its female employees, which brought her to the attention of former Governor Pete Wilson. "It was regarded as a considerable legal feat and also saved the state a ton of money," he recalled.

In 1991, he hired her as legal adviser, and then chose her as a state appeals court judge and eventually State Supreme Court justice. She has often said that she has been guided through the challenges of her life and work by her deep Christian faith, and she has often argued that judges should look to higher authorities than precedent or manmade laws in making decisions. In Sacramento, she and her mother attended the evangelical Cordova Church of Christ.

Her friends describe Justice Brown as a voracious reader, amateur poet and serious intellectual, and her speeches are filled with allusions to writers including Cicero, the apostle Paul, Abraham Lincoln, Samuel Beckett, Ayn Rand, Gertrude Himmelfarb and Friedrich von Hayek.

But she also has a fondness for rock an roll lyrics, quoting at length from Procol Harem's "Whiter Shade of Pale" in one speech and rewriting Paul Simon's song "50 Ways to Leave Your Lover" as "50 Ways to Lose Your Liberty" in another.

She once concluded a speech with, "We've had to decide before...whether to be slaves or free."

Keep your eyes on the United States' Supreme Court's view of global law. It could be one of the most telling signs of the times.

None are more hopelessly enslaved, as those who falsely believe they are free...

CHAPTER 21

My experiences in the Army have shown me that there are three types of people: sheep, shepherd and wolf.

Sheep simply graze and enjoy the fruits of the land. Their lives are fairly simplistic. Follow the lead sheep, eat the grass and sleep when necessary. The sheep are the people of this country, who simply live their lives day to day. They go to work, go to school, go shopping and then they go back home. Their thoughts are in the present and do not worry about the wolves. The shepherd is always protecting the sheep. He sacrifices his time from home, family, and friends in order to accomplish this task. Soldiers, sailors, Marines and airmen are the shepherds that protect the flock both at home and overseas.

These service members must always be vigilant and poised to protect the sheep at any moment. They cannot afford the luxury of taking a nap by a tree or leaving the flock unattended. They know that the wolf is always lurking and ready to kill a sheep when the opportunity presents itself. It is veterans like you who stood watch yesterday, which made it possible for service members like me to stand watch today and train the next generation to stand watch tomorrow.

The circle of life between sheep, shepherd, and wolf are as real today as they were for you back in the "good ol' days." The wolves I face today are Islamic terrorists. They are no more dangerous than the wolves you faced. Whether it was the North Vietnamese Army and Viet Cong in the jungles of Vietnam, the ever-assaulting waves of Korean communists or Hitler and Japan during World War II; wolves are in every generation. The shepherds of America protect not only their sheep, but also the entire world and every wolf knows it. Many shepherds have died while doing their duty. Their sacrifice is not in vain. My generation has picked up the staff and stands ready to defend just as you and your predecessors did. All of us standing here today have spent time on watch. For all of you, I sincerely wish peace and prosperity for your families and yourselves.

You have earned it. It is my time to protect the people and this country as well as train the next generation to do the same.

The above is a great article written by one of America's young military enlistees about why he serves.

Since its inception America has come under attack from many directions, but they were always frontal attacks and we knew the enemy. America is once again engaging in a life or death struggle, but our enemy today has multiple fronts and as a stealth-like adversary...represents the most sinister one yet. We have fought many military conflicts around the world and have always come out victorious because of our superior military strength. But our survival today cannot be secured by military might.

Our enemies today encompass many abstract and diverse elements, all seemingly moving in unison...almost as if choreographed. But we are our own worth enemy in that we have lost our identity along the way, we have forsaken our heritage, our values and more importantly... our God!

We are no longer "One Nation Under God," more and more we're beginning to resemble a gerrymandered collage of clans. Enclaves based on various ideologies, ethnicities, religions and other "self-serving" drivers.

I also believe that the relentlessly pervasive spread of Islam (like a plague), throughout the world, is designed to bring all countries under a global Islamic umbrella. The bigger problem here is that history tells us, that from day one...Islamic and Christianity have never been compatible neighbors. I fear that under that umbrella, America... in time, could become a tribal patchwork country like many of the Middle East countries.

I do not believe that our current president is an ally of America nor an admirer of our history or culture...and by extension, much of his staff and the liberal-progressives in his party. I also believe "he" has a deep-seated grudge against America and is determined to take it down several notches...even bankrupt it.

All the above has come together with a progressive mentality that has been growing and infecting our society for well over a hundred years. And with the full-blown emergence of "political correctness"...progressivism now has its handmaiden.

The article below was originally attributed to a commercial airline pilot with American Airlines. But in checking with "Snopes," I found it interesting that while they did, in fact, acknowledge the commentary...they could not verify the author. But, they were able to say that the "name" associated with the original circulation of the letter was/is, in fact, an employee of American Airlines. One has to wonder about the power of "political correctness" being applied here.

So with that said, I will say, "Author unknown."

The following is the letter penned by the "now unknown writer," to address a Muslim doctor's assertions/complaint that he was being profiled because he had been checked three times while boarding an airplane.

"Whoever" wrote the piece certainly spoke for a major portion of Americans. His apprehension and concerns are valid in light of the turmoil that has turned our world upside down. He spoke from the heart in sharing his fears for not only himself but also those around him. His delivery was without malice or absolutes; he was merely trying to explain why many Americans feel uncomfortable about certain elements of the Islamic culture.

His message was only to explain America's point of view:

YOU WORRY ME!

I've been trying to say this since 911; you worry me. I wish you didn't. I wish when I walk down the streets of this country that I love, that your color and culture still blended with the beautiful human landscape we enjoy in this country. But you don't blend in anymore. I notice you, and it worries me.

I notice you because I can't help it anymore. People from your homelands, professing to be Muslims, have been attacking and killing my fellow citizens and our friends for more than 20 years now. I don't fully understand their grievances and hate, but I know that nothing can justify the inhumanity of their attacks.

On September 11, Arab/Muslims hijacked four jetliners in my country. They cut the throats of women in front of children and brutally stabbed others to death. They took control of those planes and crashed them into buildings, killing thousands of proud fathers, loving sons, wise grandparents, elegant daughters, best friends, favorite coaches, fearless public servants, and children's mothers.

The Palestinians celebrated, the Iraqis were overjoyed, as was most of the Arab world. So, I notice you now. I don't want to be worried. I don't want to be consumed by the same rage, hate and prejudice that destroyed the souls of those terrorists. But I need your help. As a rational American, trying to protect my country and family in an irrational and unsafe world, I must know how to tell the difference between you, and the Arab/Muslim terrorist.

How do I differentiate between the true Arab/Muslim Americans and the Arab/Muslim terrorists in our communities who are attending our schools, enjoying our parks, and living in our communities under the protection of our constitution, while they plot the next attack that will slaughter these same good neighbors and children?

The events of September 11th changed the answer. It is not my responsibility to determine which of you embraces our great country, with all of its religions, with all of its different citizens, with all of its faults. It is time for every Arab/Muslim in this country to determine it for me.

I want to know, I demand to know and I have a right to know, whether or not you love America. Do you pledge allegiance to its flag? Do you proudly display it in front of your house, or on your car? Do you pray in your many daily prayers that Allah will bless this nation; that He will protect it and let it prosper? Or do you pray that Allah will destroy it in one of your jihads? Are you thankful for the freedom that this nation affords? A freedom that was paid for by the blood of hundreds of thousands of patriots who gave their lives for this country? Are you willing to preserve this freedom by also paying the ultimate sacrifice? Do you love America? If this is your commitment, then I need you to start letting me know about it.

Your Muslim leaders in this nation should be flooding the media at this time with hard facts on your faith, and what hard actions you are taking as a community and as a religion to protect the United States of America. Please, no more benign overtures of regret for the death of the innocent, because I worry about who you regard as innocent. No more benign overtures of condemnation for the unprovoked attacks, because I worry about what is unprovoked to you. I am not interested in any more sympathy; I am interested only in action. What will you do for America, our great country...at this time of crisis, at this time of war?

I want to see Arab/Muslims waving the American flag in the streets. I want to hear you chanting "Allah Bless America." I want to see young Arab/Muslim men enlisting in the military. I want to see a commitment of money, time and emotion to the victims of this butchering and to this nation as a whole.

The FBI has a list of over 400 people they want to talk to regarding the WTC attack. Many of these people live and socialize right now in Muslim communities. You know them. You know where they are. Hand them over to us, now! But I have seen very little approaching this sort of action. Instead I have seen an already closed and secretive community close even tighter. You have disappeared from the streets. You have posted armed security guards at your facilities. You have threatened lawsuits. You have screamed for protection from reprisals.

The very few Arab/Muslim representatives that have appeared in the media were defensive and equivocating. They seemed more concerned with making sure that the United States proves who was responsible before taking action. They seemed more concerned with protecting their fellow Muslims from violence directed towards them in the United States and abroad than they did with supporting our country and denouncing "leaders" like Khadafi, Hussein, Farrakhan, and Arafat.

If the true teachings of Islam proclaim tolerance and peace and love for all people, then I want chapter and verse from the Koran and statements from popular Muslim leaders to back it up. What good is it if the teachings in the Koran are good, pure, and true, when your "leaders" are teaching fanatical interpretations, terrorism, and intolerance? It matters little how good Islam should be if huge numbers of the world's Muslims interpret the teachings of Mohammed incorrectly and adhere to a degenerative form of the religion. A form that has been demonstrated to us over and over again. A form whose structure is built upon a foundation of violence, death, and suicide. A form whose members are recruited from the prisons around the world. A form whose members (some as young as five years old) are seen day after day, week in and week out, year after year, marching in the streets around the world, burning effigies of our presidents, burning the American flag, shooting weapons into the air. A form whose members convert from a peaceful religion, only to take up arms against the great United States of America, the country of their birth. A form whose rules are so twisted, that their traveling members refuse to show their faces at airport security checkpoints, in the name of Islam.

We will never allow the attacks of September 11, or any others for that matter, to take away that which is so precious to us...our rights under the greatest constitution in the world. I want to know where every Arab/Muslim in this country stands and I think it is my right and the right of every true citizen of this country to demand it. A right paid for by the blood of thousands of my brothers and sisters who died protecting the very constitution that is protecting you and your family.

I am pleading with you to let me know. I want you here as my brother, my neighbor, my friend, as a fellow American. But there can be no gray areas or ambivalence regarding your allegiance, and it is up to you, to show me, where you stand.

Until then, "YOU WORRY ME!"

CHAPTER 22

Rahm Emanuel cynically said, "You never want a crisis to go to waste." It is now becoming clear that the crisis he was referring to is Barack Obama's presidency.

Obama is no fool. He is not incompetent. To the contrary, he is brilliant. He knows exactly what he's doing. He is purposely overwhelming the U.S. economy to create systemic failure, economic crisis and social chaos...thereby destroying capitalism and our country from within.

Barack Obama was my college classmate (Columbia University, class of '83). As Glenn Beck correctly predicted from day one, Obama is following the plan of Cloward & Piven, two professors at Columbia University. They outlined a plan to socialize America by overwhelming the system with government spending and entitlement demands. Add up the clues below. Taken individually they're alarming. Taken as a whole, it is a brilliant, Machiavellian (the employment of cunning and duplicity) game plan to turn the United States into a socialist/Marxist state with a permanent majority that desperately needs government for survival...and can be counted on to always vote for bigger government. Why not? They have no responsibility to pay for it.

Universal health care. The health care bill had very little to do with health care. It had everything to do with unionizing millions of hospital and health care workers, as well as adding 15,000 to 20,000 new IRS agents (who will join government employee unions). Obama doesn't care that giving free health care to 30 million Americans will add trillions to the national debt. What he does care about is that it cements the dependence of those 30 million voters to Democrats and big government. Who but a socialist revolutionary would pass this reckless spending bill in the middle of a depression?

Cap and trade. Like health care legislation having nothing to do with health care, cap and trade has nothing to do with global warming. It has everything to do with the redistribution of income, government control of the economy and a criminal payoff to Obama's biggest contributors. Those powerful and wealthy unions and contributors (like GE, which owns NBC, MSNBC and CNBC) can then be counted on to support everything Obama wants. They will kickback hundreds of millions of dollars in contributions to Obama and the Democratic Party to keep them in power. The bonus is that all the new taxes on Americans with bigger cars, bigger homes and businesses help Obama "spread the wealth around."

Make Puerto Rico a state. Why? Who's asking for a 51st state? Who's asking for millions of new welfare recipients and government entitlement addicts in the middle of a depression? Certainly not American taxpayers. But this has been Obama's plan all along. His goal is to add two new Democrat senators, five Democrat congressmen and a million loyal Democrat voters who will be dependent on big government.

Legalize 12 million illegal immigrants. Just giving these 12 million potential new citizens free health care alone could overwhelm the system and bankrupt America. But it adds 12 million reliable new Democrat voters who can be counted on to support big government. Add another few trillion dollars in welfare, aid to dependent children, food stamps, free medical, education, tax credits for the poor, and eventually Social Security.

Stimulus and bailouts. Where did all that money go? It went to Democrat contributors, organizations (ACORN), and unions...including billions of dollars to save and/or create jobs for government employees across the country. It went to save GM and Chrysler so that their employees could keep paying union dues. It went to AIG so that Goldman Sachs could be bailed out (after giving Obama almost $1 million in contributions). A staggering $125 billion went to teachers (thereby protecting their union dues). All those public employees will vote loyally Democrat to protect their bloated salaries and pensions that are bankrupting America. The country goes broke, future generations face a bleak future, but Obama, the Democrat Party, government, and the unions grow more powerful. The end justifies the means.

Raise taxes on small business owners, high-income earners, and job creators. Put the entire burden on only the top 20 percent of taxpayers, redistribute the income, punish success, and reward those who did nothing to deserve it (except vote for Obama). Reagan wanted to dramatically cut taxes in order to starve the government. Obama wants to dramatically raise taxes to starve his political opposition.

With the acts outlined above, Obama and his regime have created a vast and rapidly expanding constituency of voters dependent on big government; a vast privileged class of public employees who work for big government;

and a government dedicated to destroying capitalism and installing themselves as socialist rulers by overwhelming the system.

Add it up and you've got the perfect Marxist scheme... all devised by my Columbia University college classmate Barack Obama.

He is also a devout Muslim...do not be fooled.

Wayne Allyn Root was the 2008 Libertarian Party vice presidential nominee and serves on the Libertarian National Committee.

The article above: "Correctly attributed," says Snopes!

http://www.snopes.com/politics/soapbox/overwhelm.asp

The State (big government) has had...and continues to maintain, a vested interest in promoting attitudes that would tend to make us skeptical of our own abilities, fearful of the motives of others and emotionally dependent upon external authorities for purpose and direction in our lives.

Some presidential elections are more important than others. From all indications, the one coming up on November 6, 2012 may well turn out to be one of the most significant in modern history.

America was never designed...or intended, to be a welfare state. It was aggressively hostile to the tumultuous emergence of socialism and communism during the early years of the 20th century. In retrospect, we can see that even during the contentious debates regarding key differences on programs and policies, no one of any stature on either side advanced proposals that seriously imperiled the constitutional scaffolding that holds our nation together. That is, until Barrack Obama...November 6, 2012, may well be D-Day, "the Day of Decision."

"Freedom is never more than one generation away from extinction."

Ronald Reagan

Chapter 23

I have this theory about Barack Obama. I think he has led a kind of make-believe life in which money was provided and doors were opened because at some point early on somebody or some group took a look at this tall, good looking, half-white, half-black, young man with an exotic African/Muslim name and concluded he could be guided toward a life in politics where his facile speaking skills could even put him in the White House.

In a very real way, he has been a young man in a very big hurry. Who else do you know that has written two memoirs before the age of 45? "Dreams of My Father" was published in 1995 when he was only 34 years old. The "Audacity of Hope" followed in 2006...if indeed, he did write them himself. There are some who think that his mentor and friend, Bill Ayers, a man who calls himself a "communist" with a small 'c' was the real author.

His political skills consisted of rarely voting on anything that might be deemed controversial. He went from a legislator in the Illinois legislature to the Senator from that state because he had the good fortune of having Mayor Daley's formidable political machine at his disposal.

He was in the United States Senate so briefly that his bid for the presidency was either an act of astonishing self-confidence or part of some greater game plan that had been determined before he first stepped foot into the Capital. How, many must wonder, was he selected to be a 2004 keynote speaker at the Democrat convention that nominated John Kerry when virtually no one had ever even heard of him before?

He outmaneuvered Hillary Clinton in primaries. He took Iowa by storm. A charming young man, an anomaly in the state with a very small black population, he oozed "cool" in a place where agriculture was the antithesis of cool. He dazzled the locals. And he had an army of volunteers drawn to a charisma that hid any real substance.

And then he had the great good fortune of having the Republicans select one of the most inept candidates for the presidency since Bob Dole. And then John McCain did something crazy. He picked Sarah Palin, an unknown female governor from the very distant state of Alaska. It was a ticket that was reminiscent of 1984's Walter Mondale and Geraldine Ferraro and they went down to defeat.

The mainstream political media fell in love with him. It was a schoolgirl crush with febrile commentators like Chris Mathews swooning then and now over the man. The venom directed against McCain and, in particular, Palin, was extraordinary.

Now, well into the third year of his first term, all of those gilded years leading up to the White House have left him unprepared to be President. Left to his own instincts, he has a talent for saying the wrong thing at the wrong time. It swiftly became a joke that he could not deliver even the briefest of statements without the ever-present Tele-Prompters.

Far worse, however, is his capacity to want to "wish away" some terrible realities, not the least of which is the Islamist intention to destroy America and enslave the West. Any student of history knows how swiftly Islam initially spread. It knocked on the doors of Europe, having gained a foothold in Spain.

The great crowds that greeted him at home or on his campaign "world tour" were no substitute for having even the slightest grasp of history and the reality of a world filled with really bad people with really bad intentions.

Oddly and perhaps even inevitably, his political experience, a cakewalk, has positioned him to destroy the Democrat Party's hold on power in Congress because in the end it was never about the Party. It was always about his communist ideology, learned at an early age from family, mentors, college professors, and extreme leftist friends and colleagues.

Obama is a man who could deliver a snap judgment about a Boston police officer who arrested an "obstreperous" Harvard professor-friend, but would warn Americans against "jumping to conclusions" about a mass murderer at Fort Hood who shouted "Allahu Akbar." The absurdity of that was lost on no one. He has since compounded this by calling the Christmas bomber "an isolated extremist" only to have to admit a day or two later that he was part of an al Qaeda plot.

He is a man who would strive to close down our detention facility at Guantanamo even though those released were known to have returned to the battlefield against America. He could even instruct his Attorney General to afford the perpetrator of 9/11 a civil trial when no one else would ever even consider such an obscenity. And he is a man who could wait three days before having anything to say about the perpetrator of yet another terrorist attack on

Americans and then have to elaborate on his remarks the following day because his first statement was so lame.

The pattern repeats itself. He either blames problems on the Bush administration or he naively seeks to wish away the truth.

Knock, knock; is anyone home...is anyone there? Barack Obama exists only as the sock puppet of his handlers, of the people who have maneuvered and manufactured this pathetic individual's life.

When anyone else would quickly and easily produce a birth certificate, this man has spent over a million dollars to deny access to his. Most other documents, the paper trail we all leave in our wake, have been sequestered from review. He has lived a make-believe life whose true facts remain hidden.

We laugh at the ventriloquist's dummy, but what do you do when the dummy is President of the United States of America?

At a time when many Americans can barely afford Burger King and a movie, Obama boasts of spending a billion dollars on his re-election campaign. Questioned at a recent appearance about the spiraling fuel costs, Obama said, "Get used to it"...and with an insouciant grin and chortle, he told another person at the event, who complained about the effect high fuel prices were having on his family, to "get a more fuel-efficient car."

The Obamas behave as if they were sharecroppers living in a trailer and hit the Powerball, but instead of getting new tires for their trailer and a new pickup truck, they moved to Washington. And instead of making possum pie, with goats and chickens in the front yard, they're spending and living large at taxpayer expense...opulent vacations, gala balls, resplendent dinners and exclusive command performances at the White House, grand date nights, golf, basketball, more golf, exclusive resorts and still more golf.

Expensive, ill-fitting and ill-chosen wigs and fashions hardly befit the first lady of the United States. The Obamas have behaved in every way but presidential... which is why it's so offensive when we hear Obama say, "In order to restore fiscal responsibility, we all need to share in the sacrifice." But we shouldn't have to sacrifice the America we believe in.

The American people have been sacrificing; it is he and his family who are behaving as if they've never had two nickels to rub together...and now, having hit the mother lode, they're going to spend away their feelings of inadequacy at the taxpayers' expense.

Obama continues to exhibit behavior that, at best, can be described as mobocratic and, at worst, reveals a deeply damaged individual. "Is Obama unraveling?" It would appear the growing mistrust of him and contempt for his policies is beginning to have a destabilizing effect on him.

Not having things go one's way can be a bitter pill, but reasonable people don't behave as he has been behaving. It appeared, at that time, as if he was fraying around the emotional edges. That behavior has not abated...it has become more pronounced. While addressing the nation, after being forced to explain the validity of his unilateral aggression with Libya, America witnessed a petulant individual scowling and scolding the public for daring to insist he explain his actions.

But during an afternoon speech to address the budget/debt, he took his scornful, unstable despotic behavior to depths that should give the nation cause for concern. He invited Representative Paul Ryan, R-Wisconsin, to sit in the front row during his speech and then proceeded to berate both Ryan and Ryan's budget-cutting plan. Even liberal Democrats were put off by the act. MSNBC's Joe Scarborough questioned the sanity of Obama's actions.

And of course we all remember his very public lambasting of the Supreme Court last year regarding their ruling on Campaign Financing. Like Paul Ryan, members were seated up front as Obama unloaded on them about their rendering and how wrong they were.

Obama's speech was chock full of lies, deceit and crass fear mongering. It must be said that he is the most dishonest, deceitful and mendacious person, in a position of power, that most of us have ever witnessed.

His performance was the culmination of several years of outright lies and narcissism that have been largely ignored by the media, including some in the conservative press and political class who are reluctant to call him what he is in the bluntest of terms, a liar and a fraud. That he relies on his skin color to intimidate, either outright or by insinuation against those who oppose his radical agenda only add to his audacity. It is apparent that he has gotten away with his character flaws his entire life, aided and abetted by sycophants around him.

With these being among the kinder rebukes being directed at Obama, and with people becoming less intimidated by his willingness to use race as a bludgeon, with falling poll numbers in every meaningful category and an increasingly aggressive tea-party opposition...how much longer before he cracks completely?

The coming months of political life are not going to be pleasant for Obama. Possessed by a self-perceived palatine mindset that in his mind places him above criticism, how long before he cracks in public? Can America risk a man with a documented track record of lying and misrepresenting truth as a basic way of life, who is becoming increasingly more contumelious?

CHAPTER 24

W e've all heard the old saying that even when you don't respect the man, you should respect the office. So, how does it work when the man in the office doesn't respect the office? The only protocol Obama is intimately acquainted with is a gangster mentality laced with ghetto sarcasm, ridicule and mockery...but that's mostly use when working for a bipartisan agreement with the Republicans. If he's courting southern conservative voters, protocol leans more to a folksy demeanor with a bit of humble pie dished out. In Europe it's more like I'm King and you may kiss my hand. But in the Middle East, it's please allow me to bow and kiss your hand.

Obama's Fabrications Taint His Presidency:

The White House isn't challenging a new book's account suggesting that President Barack Obama fumbled the details of a pivotal anecdote about his mother's deathbed dispute with an insurance company, according to The New York Times.

During the 2008 presidential campaign and also during the ensuing fight over the healthcare law after his election, Obama repeated a story that his mother had to battle her insurer's contention that her cancer was a pre-existing condition that disqualified her from coverage, the Times reports. He recounted the story in pushing to end insurers' pre-existing condition exclusions, leaving the impression that his mother's fight involved health benefits for medical expenses.

But author Janny Scott's book, "A Singular Woman: The Untold Story of Barack Obama's Mother," quotes correspondence between Obama's mother and Ann Dunham, indicating that the 1995 dispute involved a Cigna disability insurance policy instead of health benefits; she was turned down for disability insurance because of a pre-existing condition. Her cancer treatments were fully covered by her employer's insurance policy.

The Times had repeatedly requested White House feedback since mid-June, shortly after the book was released, and finally got a response Wednesday, when "a White House spokesman" chose not to dispute either Scott's account or Mr. Obama's memory, while arguing that Mr. Obama's broader point remained salient. But he did add that Obama's mother still had several hundred dollars a month in medical expenses that were not covered...as if any health insurance policy would pay 100 percent of medical bills.

Since he began campaigning for president, Barack Obama has claimed that because his mother had a pre-existing condition, she died of cancer without health insurance coverage.

As it turns out, that was a pure invention to win support for passage of his healthcare legislation. So too was Obama's claim that he watched at his mother's bedside as she suffered the disease without being insured.

"I remember just being heartbroken," he said in a 2007 campaign appearance, "seeing her struggle."

Moreover, Obama had not seen his mother for months before she died in a Honolulu hospital in 1995, according to Scott's book and to friends interviewed by The Washington Post. Her son was in Chicago, planning a run for an Illinois state Senate seat. He did not go to see his mother until a day after she died on November 7, 1995.

The White House spokesman did not dispute Scott's account of the above paragraph either; but added that Obama told his story based on his recollection of events that took place more than 15 years ago.

That excuse is as credible as Obama's claim that he had no idea his minister and self-described mentor, the Reverend Jeremiah Wright Jr., was an anti-white, anti-America and anti-Israel hatemonger.

Scott also recounted how Obama distorted Wright's background, "Obama went on to make up stories about how deprived and discriminated against Wright was while growing up in Philadelphia."

In fact, Wright grew up in a comfortable middle class family in a racially mixed neighborhood. He attended Central High, an elite school that admits only the most qualified students from all over the city. But the press bought every word of Obama's Wright mythology.

What kind of a person would make up stories about his mother in order to score political points? The same person who would tell the American people that he wants to cut spending when he has presided over an increase in the federal debt from 53 percent of GDP in 2009 to 72 percent this year.

In February, that same person presented Congress with a budget that increases federal debt by $10 trillion over the next decade. In April, that person rejected Republican efforts to raise the debt ceiling in return for spending cuts.

Now Obama is claiming he wants spending cuts, but he will not specify which ones beyond a pathetic $2 billion.

The disparity between Obama's words and his actions goes back to the healthcare bill. He claimed no one would lose his or her existing coverage. It turns out that was more hocus-pocus. A McKinsey & Co. survey found that nearly a third of private sector employers say they will discontinue covering their employees with health insurance because of the rising cost imposed by Obama's healthcare legislation.

One reason for the increased cost is the requirement that health insurers cover everyone regardless of whether they have a pre-existing condition. That is like allowing drivers to go without car insurance and then letting them sign up for it to pay for an accident that has already occurred. The rest of the country foots the bill.

In addressing the nation's scary increased debt, Senate minority leader Mitch McConnell has accused Obama of engaging in smoke and mirrors. "Dealing with Obama is like negotiating with Jell-O," House Speaker John Boehner has said.

Looking at Obama's fabrications about his mother's illness, we can see why.

Like Barack Hussein Obama II, I am a graduate of Harvard Law School. I too have Muslims in my family. I am black, and I was once a leftist Democrat. Since our backgrounds are somewhat similar, I perceive something in Obama's policy toward Israel, which people without that background may not see. All my life I have witnessed a strain of anti-Semitism in the black community. It has been fueled by the rise of the Nation of Islam and Louis Farrakhan, but it predates that organization.

We heard it in Jesse Jackson's "HYMIE town" remark years ago during his presidential campaign. We heard it most recently in Jeremiah Wright's remark about "them Jews" not allowing Obama to speak with him. I hear it from my own Muslim family members who see the problem in the Middle East as a "Jew" problem.

Growing up in a small, predominantly black urban community in Pennsylvania, I heard the comments about Jewish shop owners. They were "greedy cheaters" who could not be trusted, according to my family and others in the neighborhood. I was too young to understand what it means to be Jewish, or know that I was hearing anti-Semitism. These people seemed nice enough to me, but others said they were "evil." Sadly, this bigotry has yet to be eradicated from the black community.

In Chicago, the anti-Jewish sentiment among black people is even more pronounced because of the direct influence of Farrakhan and the Nation of Islam. Most African Americans are not followers of "The Nation," but many have a quiet respect for its leader because, they say, "he speaks the truth" and "stands up for the black man." What they mean of course is that he viciously attacks the perceived "enemies" of the black community...white people and Jews. Even some self-described Christians buy into his demagoguery.

The question is whether Obama, given his Muslim roots and experience in Farrakhan's Chicago, shares this antipathy for Israel and Jewish people. Is there any evidence that he does? First, a virulent anti-Semite, the Reverend Jeremiah Wright, taught the President for twenty years. In the black community it is called "sitting under." You don't merely attend a church, you "sit under" a Pastor to be taught and mentored by him. Obama "sat under" Wright for a very long time. He was comfortable enough with Farrakhan, Wright's friend...to attend and help organize his "Million Man March." I was on C-Span the morning of the march arguing that we must never legitimize a racist and anti-Semite, no matter what "good" he claims to be doing. Yet a future President was in the crowd giving Farrakhan his enthusiastic support.

The classic left wing view is that Israel is the oppressive occupier, and the Palestinians are Israel's victims. Obama is clearly sympathetic to this view. In speaking to the Muslim World, he did not address the widespread Islamic hatred of Jews. Instead he attacked Israel over the growth of West Bank settlements. Surely he knows that settlements are not the crux of the problem. The absolute refusal of the Palestinians to accept Israel's right to exist as a Jewish state is the insurmountable obstacle. That's where the pressure needs to be placed, but this President sees it differently. He also made the preposterous comparison of the Holocaust to Palestinian "dislocation."

Obama clearly has Muslim sensibilities. He sees the world and Israel from a Muslim perspective. His construct of "The Muslim World" is unique in modern diplomacy. It is said that only The Muslim Brotherhood and other radical elements of the religion use that concept. It is a call to unify Muslims around the world. It is rather odd to hear an American President use it. In doing so he reveals more about his thinking than he intends. The dramatic policy reversal of joining the unrelentingly anti-Semitic, anti-Israel and pro-Islamic, United Nations' Human Rights Council is in keeping with the President's truest, albeit undeclared...sensibilities.

Those who are paying attention and thinking about these issues do not find it unreasonable to consider that President Obama is influenced by a strain of anti-Semitism picked up from the black community, his leftist friends and colleagues, his Muslim associations and his long period of mentor-ship under Jeremiah Wright. If this conclusion is accurate, Israel has some dark days ahead. For the first time in her history, she may find the President of the United States siding with her enemies. Those who believe, as I do, that Israel must be protected, had better be ready for the fight.

E. W. Jackson is Bishop of Exodus Faith Ministries, an author and retired attorney.

If a nation expects to be both ignorant and free, it expects what never was and never will be.

CHAPTER 25

We should have realized it was coming. When the United States' administration joined the call for Hosni Mubarak's ouster last winter, everyone who warned about the rise of the Muslim Brotherhood was told that it was so weak and small that its influence on the Egyptian political landscape would be inconsequential. Both the President and the Secretary of State scoffed at the idea that the Brotherhood was anything to worry about.

Remember all those "shovel ready" projects the President promised to fund with his stimulus packages? Later, he admitted that there really wasn't any such thing as a shovel ready project. But the money was already spent. Well, as Yogi Berra once said, "It's deja vu all over again."

Last week, the Secretary of State tacitly acknowledged that the Muslim Brotherhood is, indeed, a force to be reckoned with. In fact, the Brotherhood is the only organization she specifically named when she invited "all" Egyptian parties that are peaceful, and committed to non-violence...to talk with us. This administration backtracks so much the "moonwalk" should be its official dance.

Of course, the Secretary's invitation to the Muslim Brotherhood makes the President's friend and mentor, George Soros, happy. He's a supporter of Mohamed El Baradei, the former recalcitrant head of the International Atomic Energy Agency. El Baradei sits on the boards of several Soros foundations and organizations. He also seems to have the Brotherhood's backing in his run for the presidency of Egypt. And Soros and the Muslim Brotherhood share similar views of America, the Great Satan, and Israel, the Little Satan...both of which must be destroyed for their world visions to be realized.

Iran has announced that it is normalizing relations with Egypt. The late Egyptian President Anwar Sadat broke off diplomatic relations with Iran when the Iranian students occupied the United States' embassy in Tehran. He also welcomed the deposed Shah of Iran to exile in Egypt. The acts of supporting the United States during that crisis, befriending the Shah, and signing a peace treaty with Israel were more than the Muslim Brotherhood could bear, so they arranged Sadat's assassination in 1981.

Unfortunately for the Brotherhood, Mubarak survived and succeeded Sadat. He outlawed the Brotherhood and refused to restore relations with Iran. Finally, after 30 years and the help of the United States, the Muslim Brotherhood has gotten its revenge. Both Sadat and Mubarak are gone, Iran is a friend again, and Egypt is well on its way to becoming a theocracy like Iran. By the way, another American President helped Iranian Muslims achieve their goals back in 1979 (yes, another Democrat...Jimmy Carter). That hasn't turned out too good for the world, either.

What's up with the United Nations? Just when you think those buffoons over on the East River can't get any wackier; they get wackier! You'll never believe the choices they've made to fill some of the more important chairs in the United Nations' pantheon of organizations; all seemingly weighted toward benefiting "The Muslim World."

I wasn't going to elaborate on the about paragraph but it's so unbelievably ridiculous that I can't leave it hanging. Women's Rights is one of the many Councils, Committees and other ineffective organizations that constitute the United Nations. With that said; the United Nations... with its infamous wisdom, recently loaded the Women's Rights Council with Muslim men. But of course, one could facetiously point out that who could have been better qualified...and more intimately acquainted with the extensive problem of abused women. But seriously, it's a mockery...and a travesty. We've known for years that the United Nations is corrupt, but it appears that there are no limits to their corruption that power and money can't overcome.

Here's something else you may have a hard time believing. This week, the Palestinian Authority announced that it is willing to make a concession! Mark this date because it may be a historical first. I can't seem to remember the Palestinian Authority ever making a concession. The only concessions I can recall are the ones Israeli made.

Apparently, the Palestinian Authority is willing to suspend its efforts to coerce the United Nations into recognizing it as an independent nation. Wow, that's a relief. Just think of all the nasty sovereignty issues that could then be avoided. There is, however, one minor condition. All the Palestinians want is for Israel to withdraw from the territories captured in 1967 (and later) and return control of east Jerusalem to them. Once that has been done, then the Israeli-Palestinian peace talks can begin in earnest.

That's a little like a prize fight that begins with one boxer face down on the mat and the referee halfway to ten in his count.

So, to put this into perspective, the "the powers that be" are trying to bring Hamas and Fatah together into one, giant, globally-dependent terrorist state dedicated to eradicating Israel. And then, in total defiance of all logic and history, having granted them independent statehood, the United Nations hopes that they will suddenly and inexplicably change their ideology (who they are), abandon terror, and create a peaceful, industrious and prosperous society living side by side with Israel.

That's pure madness of course, but it's exactly the madness the prophets predicted for the final days before the return of Christ.

The Israeli military has issued a report that says that Hezbollah now has more than 50,000 missiles for use in its coming attack on Israel. Scattered and hidden throughout Lebanon, the arsenal is larger than that of many nations. This represents an unbelievable threat to the Jewish nation.

So what has America decided to do upon learning about this threat that looms over our Middle East ally? The logical thing of course...well, logical for the Obama Administration. The Department of Homeland Security (DHS) has placed Israel on a special watch list of 36 nations that have "a tendency to promote, produce, or protect terrorist organizations or their members." That means that visitors from these countries, including Israel, will be subjected to special treatment by US authorities. If detained by Immigration and Customs personnel, they will undergo a special security screening called a "Third Agency check."

To be fair, DHS explains that Israel is on that list because Muslim terror groups like Hamas, Islamic Jihad, and others are located inside the nation's boundaries. On the surface, that may seem logical. In reality though, Israel has suffered more than anyone else because of those terrorist organizations and the thousands of terror attacks perpetrated by these groups. And now, Israelis are suffering again because of them.

But of course we all know they were placed on the list because of pressure exerted from the political correctness balcony.

As things wind down and the prophetic scenario for the final days of this Age comes into sharper focus, it's good to know there is a way of escape. Jesus Christ provided it through His atoning sacrifice on the Cross. All we have to do is accept the gift of free pardon that His death and resurrection provides. Do it today.

Psalm 109:8

English Standard Version (ESV):

May his days be few; may another take his office!

"If we ever forget that we're one nation under GOD, then we will be a nation gone under."

Ronald Reagan

CHAPTER 26

B ecause I covered it very thoroughly in my preceding book (We the People), I haven't written much about the spread of Islam and the Muslim culture throughout the world...and especially the inundating of Europe. We are currently just seeing the first waves of "The Muslim World" tsunami. But Europe is experiencing extreme "growing pains" and even political correctness can't calm the impending storms on the horizon. If you remember, earlier in this book I quoted Germany's Chancellor Angela Merkel admitting that Germany's multiculturalism had "utterly failed" and they were not an anomaly... but the norm throughout Europe. She had the courage to speak out in spite of political correctness' muzzle.

But our lawmakers don't have the fortitude or desire at this early stage of the game. So like Europe did, we've closed our eyes to our impending doom while remaining naively optimistic about America's chances that our multicultural endeavor will have a happy ending.

We just never get it...that little thing about history repeating itself. What makes this even more unbelievable is that we're looking at the history of this failure even as we're moving forward with duplicating it. It's not like it's medieval history...we're looking at the failure in real time. The game is rigged, the deck stacked...the playing field is not level, but we're staying in the game. The Muslim World is already thinking, "Checkmate!" They know it's just a matter of time, and that time is on their side. They've waited hundreds of years; a few more decades matter not.

Perhaps in a preview of things to come, the self-described perpetrator of one of the worst modern mass murders in peacetime told Norwegian authorities that he now expects to spend the rest of his life in prison. He also said that two other cells of his terror network remain free.

Peaceful, liberal Norway has been stunned by the bombing in downtown Oslo and the shooting massacre at a youth camp outside the capital, which the suspect said were intended to start a revolution to inspire Norwegians to retake their country from Muslims and other immigrants.

Anders Behring Breivik has admitted bombing Norway's capital and opening fire on a "Socialist youth group retreat," but he entered a plea of not guilty, saying he wanted to save Europe from Muslim immigration. He blames liberals for championing multiculturalism over Norway's "indigenous culture."

[Referencing Chapter 19: Part 2: Obama plans to use the Obamas' nonprofit group (Public Allies), which he features on his campaign website, as the model for a national service corps. He calls his program, "Universal Voluntary Public Service." Interestingly enough though, those "volunteers" would (amongst other things) be required to attend weekly training workshops and "three retreats." And make no mistake, George Soros (Chapters 25 and 29) is driving and funding these socialist youth group retreats...worldwide.]

"The operation was not to kill as many people as possible but to give a strong signal, that could not be misunderstood, that as long as the Labor Party keeps driving its ideological lies and deconstructing the Norwegian culture...and facilitating the mass importation of Muslims," then they must assume responsibility for this treason," Breivik stated in court.

Breivik made it clear, in an Internet manifesto that he planned to turn his court appearance into theater, preparing a speech for his appearance in court even before launching the attacks, then requesting an open hearing in which he would wear a uniform. Both of those requests have been denied.

In that same online manifesto published shortly before Friday's attack, Breivik styled himself as a Christian conservative fighting against Marxist conspiracies and the perceived Muslim colonization of Europe.

The suspect stated that "he staged the bombing and the Socialist youth camp rampage as marketing for his manifesto calling for a revolution that would rid Europe of Muslims."

His reason (for the attacks) was that he wanted to start a war against democracy, against the Muslims in the world, and as he said he wanted to liberate Europe and the Western world. He saw himself as a warrior and savior of the Western world.

Prosecutor Christian Hatlo told reporters that Breivik was very calm and seemed unaffected by what has happened. He said Breivik told investigators during his interrogation that he never expects to be released.

Police said Breivik used two weapons during the rampage...both of which were bought legally, according to the manifesto. A doctor treating victims told The Associated Press that the gunman used illegal "dum-dum"-style bullets...bullets designed to disintegrate inside the body and cause maximum internal damage.

Below are three brief excerpts from his manifesto that illustrate the nature of his writing and his obsessions:

> "I have spent several years writing, research-ing and compiling the information and I have spent most of my hard-earned funds (in excess of 300,000 Euros) in the process. I do not want any compensation for it as it is a gift to you, as a fellow patriot."

> "In order to successfully penetrate the cultural Marxist/multiculturalist media censorship we are forced to employ significantly more brutal and breath taking operations which will result in casu-alties. In order for the attack to gain an influential effect, assassinations and the use of weapons of mass destruction must be embraced."

> "The ideology that has taken over Western Europe goes most commonly by the name of 'Political Correctness.' Some people see it as a joke. It is not a joke. It is deadly serious. It seeks to alter virtu-ally all the rules, formal and informal, that govern relations among people and institutions. It wants to change our behavior, our thoughts...even the words we use."

The head of the world's largest ecumenical group ac-cused Norwegian gunman Anders Behring Breivik of blasphemy Monday for citing Christianity as a justifica-tion in his murderous attack on government buildings and a youth camp that left dozens dead.

Following a wave of near universal revulsion against the attacks, a secondary wave began developing that seemed to build as more and more people spoke up with statements that appeared to defend the extremist views, which drove the Norwegian gunman to carry out the massacre.

Stephen Lennon, leader of the English Defense League, told The Associated Press on Tuesday that he does not condone Breivik's rampage but "the facts are that many people are scared...and governments are not listening to them. What happened in Oslo shows how desperate some people are becoming in Europe. It's a ticking time bomb. If they don't give that frustration and anger a platform and a voice...a way of getting emotions out in a democratic way, it will create monsters like this lunatic."

Lennon said, "The English Defense League was founded two years ago when British troops returned from Afghanistan, to insults and harassment from Muslims in Luton, a town outside of London where the radical Islamic preacher, Abu Hamza al-Masri...the one-eyed, hook-handed cleric, used to preach occasionally."

The group says it wants peace, but it also wants an end to Islamic immigration, Shariah law and building mosques "until Islam sorts itself out," Lennon said. He went on to say that there are other groups across Europe that feel the same way. "Islam is a threat to Europe," he said, denying that he is against cross-culturalism or Muslims. "People should look at what happened in Oslo and understand that there is growing anger in Europe. You suppress people's rights, you suppress people's voices and people will just continue to go <u>underground</u>."

The Northern League, the junior partner in Premier Silvio Berlusconi's government, has caused a stir with its increasingly virulent anti-immigrant, anti-Islamic rhetoric.

Meanwhile, Mario Borghezio, a European parliamentarian who belongs to Italy's populist Northern League party, told a mainstream Italian radio station that he sympathized with some of Breivik's ideas. He also said, "Some of the ideas he expressed are good, and barring the violence...some of them are great."

The act of such deadly right-wing terrorism stunned a continent that has been grappling with a wave of xenophobia and anti-immigrant violence amid faltering economies, rising unemployment, and ongoing fears about Islamic terror plots.

I find it interesting how political correctness seems spun to work for Islam while Christianity is on its own.

"Jerry Springer: The Opera" is a British musical written by Richard Thomas and Stewart Lee, based on the television show "The Jerry Springer Show." The musical is notable for its profanity, its irreverent treatment of Judeo-Christian themes, and surreal images such as a troupe of tap-dancing Ku Klux Klan members. The spoof included, among others...God, Jesus, Mary, Adam and Eve and Satan.

Yes, there was some localized protecting by Christians... but they were peaceful.

But had that lampoon been about Allah, the prophet Muhammed and Islam, there would have been big problems...around the world.

In looking back (history again), I can recall the 1988 death threats against Salman Rushdie for writing "Satanic Verses" and the 2004 murder of Dutch film director Theo Van Gogh for publicly opposing Islam with voice and film. Then there's the 2005 riots and deaths after the Danish newspaper Jyllands-Posten published

12 caricatures of Muhammad; the 2009 prosecution of Dutch parliamentarian Geert Wilders for statements they deemed "insulting and harmful to the religious esteem of Muslims"...and the 2009 cancellation of events at both Columbia and Princeton which were to have featured Nonie Darwich, co-founder of Former Muslims United.

The reintroduction of Sharia is a longstanding goal for Islamist movements in Muslim countries. Some Muslim minorities in Asia have maintained institutional recognition of Sharia to adjudicate their personal and community affairs. In western countries, where Muslim immigration is more recent, Muslim minorities have introduced Sharia family law, for use in their own disputes, with varying degrees of success (Britain's Muslim Arbitration Tribunal). Attempts to impose Sharia have been accompanied by controversy, violence, and even warfare (Second Sudanese Civil War).

The Center for Security Policy's report, Shariah Law and American State Courts: An Assessment of State Appellate Court Cases, that involved conflicts between Shariah (Islamic law) and American state law, revealed the evaluation of 50 Appellate Court cases from 23 states.

These cases are the stories of Muslim American families, mostly Muslim women and children, who were asking American courts to preserve their rights to equal protection and due process. These families came to America for freedom from the discriminatory and cruel laws of Shariah. When our courts then apply Shariah law in the lives of these families, and deny them equal protection, they are betraying the principles on which America was founded.

Recent studies are finding and/or suggesting that Shariah law has entered into state court decisions, in conflict with the Constitution and state public policy. Some commentators have said there are no more than one or two cases of Shariah law playing out in any of America's state court cases; yet research has exposed 50 significant cases just from the small sample of appellate published cases.

Others have asserted with certainty that state court judges will always reject any foreign law, including Shariah law, when it conflicts with the Constitution or state public policy; yet once again...researchers found 15 Trial Court cases, and 12 Appellate Court cases, where Shariah was found to be applicable in those particular cases. The facts are the facts; some judges are making decisions deferring to Shariah law even when those decisions conflict with Constitutional protections.

Again, we are being asked...is our Constitution becoming irrelevant?

Some Americans argue that the United States civil and criminal legal codes and courts should recognize Islamic law (Shariah), as applied to Muslim families, at least. But Shariah critics need point no further than Australia to show the utter incoherence of that contention.

Polygamy is illegal in Australia, as is marriage of underage women and children.

Nevertheless, Australia accepts "valid Muslim polygamist marriages, lawfully entered into overseas, with second and third wives and their children able to claim welfare and other benefits," according to The Australian legal affairs editor Chris Merritt. Australia accepts them, even though in many such marriages the female is "under Australia's lawful marriage age."

In effect, Australia has allowed a parallel legal system, operating against its own statutes as a sort of illegal "shadow system"...to take hold.

Courts and attorneys down under may be largely "oblivious," but Shariah has taken root there, according to legal research by academics Ann Black and Kerrie Sadie. Their findings are due to be published July 25th, in the New South Wales Law Journal. In a 2008 survey, they found that 90 percent of Australian Muslims adhere to its civil laws and rejected Shariah.

Yet the researchers also found that, under the radar, many Australian Muslims have also long observed Islamic traditions and Shariah, particularly in family matters. Not all Australian Muslims register new marriages taking place there. Since Islamic law endorses polygamous and underage marriages, some families seal marital vows solely with religious ceremonies, breaching Australia's Marriage Act. A man may take multiple wives and it matters not if any...or all, of those wives are below the legal age at which Australia allows men and women to marry.

The Australian Muslim push for broad acceptance of Shariah has not occurred in a vacuum, however. In North America, the United States and Canadian Muslim organizations and leaders are also campaigners for the adaptation of Shariah laws in as many venues as possible...as they press on for Western legalization of polygamy for Muslims.

Islam does not require second wives, so while Muslims in the West are not required to take multiple wives, they claim that Western prohibition of second wives for Muslims denies "a particular right according to Shariah." Their ultimate goal is America's acknowledgement of Shariah law. They often claim that for men with barren wives "instinctively aspiring to have children or heirs," or "chronically ill" wives that polygamy is the best solution. Otherwise they must divorce or forever "suppress their instinctive sexual needs" or even secretly take "one or more illicit sex partners." Forget women's wants or needs...polygamy is an "optional solution."

Clerics at the Assembly of Muslim Jurists of America likewise extol Shariah-endorsed polygamy. AMJA currently encourages Muslim Americans to engage in polygamous marriages in the United States, where polygamous marriages, in every state of the union, remain completely and totally illegal.

In early August 2007, the AMJA clerics stated that as long as you don't register and/or record your marriage, it is okay to have more than one wife here in the states. A questioner argued that since the law prohibits marriage to more than one female at a time, isn't it against Shariah...and if so, is it okay for us to break that law? In essence, he asked whether Islam makes it legal or forbidden to abide by U.S. law.

The cleric replied in favor of Islam (emphasis added):

Polygamy is permissible in Islam and may be highly recommended when the number of females is larger than that of males to afford all females a decent life that suffices their physiologic, emotional and other needs. The US law about polygamy is against the Islamic law, for no one can make prohibited that which Allah specifically made allowable.

A Muslim should respect U.S. laws on polygamy, the cleric suggested, but only so as not to harm the reputations of either polygamy or Muslims, or harm his community or family, including the second partner and her children from him. Since many celebrities have extramarital affairs and are not prosecuted, he concluded that America has a double standard when it comes to Muslims.

In October 2007, AMJA cleric Main Khalid Al-Qudah approved a Muslim's request for Islamic validation of polygamy in another religious ruling (fatwa 2134).

Polygamy, he wrote: is permissible for different reasons, like:

➢ The sexual energy of men is more than that of women in general. So, in some cases, one wife is not enough to fulfill the conjugal desire of her husband.

➢ Pregnancy and delivery negatively affect the shape and physical attraction that women have.

➢ World wide, the percentage of females is always more than that of males, eventually, there must be a solution, either to permit adultery and prostitution, or to allow polygamy.

➢ One husband could take care of more than one wife at the same time, socially, financially, and even sexually as I mentioned above. However, the opposite is not right because of the physical and psychological capability that Allah the all mighty gave men.

And while there is a more radically extreme component to Shariah, I don't feel the need...or the desire to wade into that chasm.

Anyone who thinks "a little bit of Shariah is okay" should think a little deeper. A little bit of Shariah is akin to being "a little bit" pregnant.

Our nation must consider whether its Constitution and laws...or a hodgepodge of regional, self-serving laws, should govern its population.

Once Shariah is "a little bit accepted," there is no going back. That explains, moreover, why Muslim clerics would like nothing better than to "introduce us" to Shariah "a little bit" at a time.

Shariah vs. U.S law:

Shariah Law is a "strict set of regulations." From the highest-regarded Muslim authorities like Sheik Yusef al-Qaradawi, to the authoritative Islamic manual, "Reliance of the Traveler: The Classic Manuel of Islamic Sacred Law Umdat Al-Salik," to renowned historical scholars like Bernard Lewis, there is consensus that Shariah is a body of religious laws interpreted and applied by clerics. Shariah law recognizes no authoritative secular source of law and no inalienable individual rights. Certainly, not all Muslims in the United States are Shariah-adherent, but recent surveys affirm that most who attend mosque are.

If America is to avoid the parallel Shariah societies that threaten the United Kingdom and France, we must confront this anti-constitutional system and deny it official status within our consensually organized, constitutionally ordered society.

The United Kingdom, now with 85 Shariah courts and communities displaying warning signs announcing areas as Shariah Zones, has officially announced that the government will no longer engage with or fund groups that fail to uphold "universal human rights, equality before the law, democracy and full participation in our society."

There is legislation under consideration to establish British law as transcendent. French courts deny Shariah-based family law arrangements. It is time that the United

States recognizes that Shariah and our Constitution are on a collision course.

"Good people do not need laws to tell them to act responsibly, while bad peoples will find a way around the laws."

Plato

CHAPTER 27

For dominant powers in decline, it always starts with the money, for Washington as for London and Rome before it. But it never stops there. The horizons shrivel. Two-bit provocateurs across the map pick off remnants of the old order with ever-greater ease.

America has had two roles in a so-called "globalized" world: America's government was the guarantor of global order; America's economy was the engine of global prosperity. Right now, both roles are up for grabs. And there are no takers for the former. "Life on this planet...as we know it today, is going to change, and very fast."

The pending selection of a Republican presidential candidate to challenge Barack Obama is gathering steam. The outcome will be critical in determining our future, to a degree not yet fully appreciated by a largely unaware public.

The two major parties are on a collision course whose conclusion will be the culmination of a series of events that began over 75 years ago, all seemingly impelled by the best of good intentions.

As I've stated before, America was never designed to be a welfare state. The Great Depression in the 1930s, however, gave President Franklin Delano Roosevelt the chance to expand like never before the role, the powers...and, therefore, the size and incursions, of the federal government into the social, economic and political fabric of our society.

The resultant political rewards, reaped by Roosevelt and his party...in the voting booth, were not lost on those who followed him.

Lyndon Johnson doubled down, and then some...on FDR's forays into social activism. Suddenly, the federal government declared its intention to create the Great Society, and to undertake a War on Poverty.

The liberal approach...devising a government remedy for every real or imagined social ill...went into high gear. The subtle conversion from self-reliance to governmental dependency was a tectonic shift.

Among other things, with the advent of a variety of welfare programs, they became the primary attraction, rather than freedom and opportunity, for immigrants seeking to come here.

Enter Ronald Reagan:

Ronald Reagan shaped a new popular understanding of conservatism, emphasizing its strong appeal in terms of traditional American values. He argued tirelessly that a power-hungry central government crushes our independence, stifles free enterprise, and inevitably makes us overly dependent on government.

Conservatism as a more sharply defined political philosophy emerged during that time, and has been steadily gaining traction ever since.

But then along came Obama:

Here is a man who unabashedly declared his intent to bring about a "fundamental transformation" of this country; a man who expressed his impatience that "the Supreme Court never ventured into the issues of redistribution of wealth and the more basic issues of political and economic justice in this society"; a man who faulted the Warren court, generally considered to be the most liberal ever, for failing to "break free from the essential constraints that were placed by the Founding Fathers and the Constitution."

And most of all, here is a man who believes the Constitution is deficient because it states, "what the federal government can't do to you, but doesn't say what the federal government or state government must do on your behalf."

In response to the threat these ideas pose to our traditional values, a shock wave of alarm has been gathering momentum, rippling and rising through the grass roots of this country. It has become apparent that the form of radical liberalism first propagated by FDR, cultivated and nourished by LBJ and Jimmy Carter, has now mutated into a "transformative" movement seeking to convert our rapidly eroding independence into an ever-expanding dependency on our federal government.

If Obama were to be reelected, it would provide a national stamp of approval for his roadmap, wherever that may lead.

His defeat would signal its rejection.

It seems to be a reality of human nature that political movements find their essence and their voice more in response to what they are against rather than what they are for.

It would be ironic if history someday credited Barack Obama with being the pivotal figure responsible for the coming of Age of Conservatism.

Then the liberals could have their own conspiracy theory, instead of always accusing conservatives of concocting conspiracy theories.

But having said that, I do believe there's a covert effort backed by the United Nations to create a New World Order that would redistribute wealth and centralize the world's leadership.

Conspiracy theories are theories of illegitimate power, so they proliferate among people who feel powerless.

As far out as some theories may seem, there's a place where they often intersect with mainstream political thought.

Some Republicans think Obama was born in Hawaii, though they understand why others are skeptical. But we share the beliefs that socialism and multiculturalism are eating away at the moral fiber of the country, and that Obama is pushing socialist policies.

I don't think it's a grand conspiracy...a conspiracy implies some secret chamber where plots are being hatched. I think the effort to spread socialism here is an open book, and it's openly going on. If we don't reverse it, it could lead to the country's demise.

I agree with those who believe there's a concerted effort to accommodate Muslims, Latinos and other minorities that could be destructive, if not properly facilitated.

I think too many people are so bent on being fair to everybody; it's eroding the things that made America great. I personally see a need for fewer entitlements and more personal responsibility.

When cultures come together (without assimilating), things can only go one way...the ways of the Balkans (civil wars). But in Obama's utopian world we would all live hormonally together as a village...and big government would take care of everyone's needs with money taken from the few who are still contributing.

Assimilation...don't worry about that, Americans are very tolerant people. Oh, and about your various religions and culturally specific laws...not to worry, we'll give you waivers and exemptions. You know, the same way this administration has given out thousands of waivers and exemptions from its much-vaunted Obamacare health program.

Our schools are brainwashing our kids every day and our mainstream media is useless to either sides. The liberals' views are just being validated (without questioning) while the conservatives' views are being demeaned without substantiation. The only place I get my information is the Internet, my multiple inside sources and immigration reform groups. We have to combat basic evil and treason.

Radical Muslims and Latinos are being appointed to influential positions by Obama and others liberals/progressives, and that could pose a serious threat down the road.

And how do I respond to those who think I'm nuts?

"If I'm nuts, perhaps you're unfamiliar with reality and the truth."

CHAPTER 28

We've long known where the mainstream media stands...politically. But with the Obama administration it's so blatant that it's like..."here, in your face conservatives." They portray the Tea Party as an extreme-fringe-group made up solely of a bunch of racist, White bigots. Whatever it takes to keep "their man in charge" until he can complete his assigned mission. The media has never mentioned that America actually has conservative, Republicans Blacks. Who knew...?

Time to pull the cloak of invisibility off of Black conservatives:

CNN traveled with us on the Tea Party Express, to approximately 40 rallies nationwide. I, a black conservative, opened each rally singing my "American Tea Party Anthem." And yet...neither I, nor any of the other blacks on our team were seen in the CNN documentary; thus, causing viewers to conclude the Tea Party Movement is a "white thing."

For the most part, the liberal media ignores black conservatives. And when they do interview one of us, it is from a, "Can you believe this stupid Uncle Tom," point of view.

Unfortunately, conservative media and most tea party organizers do not seem to grasp the strategic wisdom in featuring and supporting black conservatives.

Brothers and sisters, the Left is exploiting Obama's skin color for everything it is worth. Their guy in the indestructible black coat of armor is making all of their liberal dreams come true; usurping more power than any "White" president could imagine in his wildest dreams.

You can't say "no" to Obama. He's Black! All opposition is racist. Folks, the left is fighting to win, working the "black thing" to the hilt. We cannot afford to leave our black weapons of mass influence on the sidelines.

Our economy is an unprecedented disaster. Pundits are saying that under "normal conditions" the president would be fired. However, they believe Obama will be re-elected. "Normal conditions" means the president would be white. In other words, pundits believe Obama's black skin is the ultimate trump card deflating all opposition to his systematic destruction of America.

Patriots, a second Obama term is the end of America as we know it.

Meanwhile, black conservatives are giving it their all, tirelessly fighting to defeat Obama, for the most part, in anonymity.

We have many great black conservatives on our side. They should be featured front and center at our rallies, TV shows, radio shows and etc, not for the sake of black conservatives, but in defense of our Tea Party Movement.

Here's how a black radio talk show host began his interview with me, "If they (meaning White tea partiers) want to attract black people, the least credible thing they could do is to stick a black guy out front wearing a cowboy hat (meaning me)."

I wanted to say, "Screw you and end the interview." But, a still small voice in my brain said, "Hang in the there." I boldly espoused conservative principles. His scheduled 10-minute radio interview with me went for 30 minutes. Remarkably, every caller into the program agreed with me. Praise God! Folks, we have got to take our message to the black community.

Also, funding should be targeted to take our Tea Party message to the black community. Seasoned politicians say nothing gets votes like going to the people; knocking on doors and showing up at community events.

Obama and his minions including the liberal media continue to lie about the intentions of the tea party. In a soon to be released book, Obama says the tea party is motivated by race. It's time we go to the black community and tell our side of the story, the truth. Let black America know the tea party has nothing to do with race and everything to do with preserving our freedom, liberty and culture.

I am trying to launch a mini tour to black colleges titled, "Reach Your Dreams." The message of my rallies targeted to black youths is, "The best route to reaching your dreams is conservatism." The rallies will feature mostly black conservative speakers including a few black conservative rappers. I will emcee, speak and sing. I need sponsorship.

Two of my buddies, Joe the Plumber and Kevin Jackson have launched their tour designed to deal with the "race" issue. Please support them folks financially and with your presence at their events. Again, not for them, but for America. Black conservatives should be flying all over the country speaking, performing and singing at tea party events.

Patriots, I am not whining or asking you to feel sorry for black conservatives. Heaven forbid, I am not. All I am saying is the Left is exploiting Obama's race "big time," destroying America, while aggressively pounding the drum more than ever that the Tea Party is racist. Meanwhile, we have powerful black resources not being maximized.

Black Conservatives are valiantly fighting along side our fellow white patriots in the Tea Party Movement. It is time to rip away the cloak of invisibility.

By Lloyd Marcus, a Black member of the Tea Party.

Who is this man residing in the White House? We know that he came from out of nowhere, selling his Hope and Change distortion of the truth...and promising the most transparent administration ever. Approaching three years now, and the only transparency is that we are now seeing what we got.

When pushing Obamacare, the president was a master of vagueness. I would describe it as, "Give me a bunch of money, and we'll figure out the details later." When reporters began asking questions regarding the fundamental makeup of "his" healthcare package, "he"...with a straight face, said, "We'll have to pass the bill to see what's in it."

But during the debit-ceiling impasse he has exceeded his already unbelievable vagueness.

Barack Obama has repeatedly posed as "the grownup in the room" and positioned himself for credit by calling participants to the White House. And each time Republicans offer a plan; he rejects it with harsh criticism. However, other than restricting corporate airplane depreciation and wanting higher taxes, Americans have virtually no idea of what he wants.

President Barack Obama addressed the nation from the East Room of the White House, July 25, 2011, on the approaching debt limit deadline.

Unfortunately, informed public policy has to reflect specific proposals. Absent concrete details, where the devil lurks, no one can adequately compare alternatives. So when the president insists on his way but refuses to offer details, we must ask, why.

Like car salesmen, politicians strive to present their wares as attractively as possible. Unlike salesmen, however, politicians' product lines consist of asserted future consequences of proposals, and the "customers" they face are far more ignorant about the merchandise than those spending their own money.

These differences explain why politicians' "sales pitches" are so vague. However, whenever vague proposals or no proposals are the best politicians publicly offer, their positions are almost certainly inadequate.

If rhetoric is unmatched by specifics, there is no reliable way to determine the consequences of an asserted plan. Only knowing the details can reveal the actual incentives facing the decision-makers involved, which is the only way to predict results, including the myriad of unintended consequences. Absent that information, promises and claims are no more than hot air.

It may be that, as with Obamacare, the president knows too little of his "solution" to provide specific plans. If so, he knows too little to deliver on his promises. Achieving those intended goals, would then necessarily...depend on blind faith that Obama and the panoply of future bureaucrats, legislators, overseers and commissions will somehow adequately grasp the entirety of the situation, know precisely what to do about it and do it right. But that is a prospect that due to the painful lessons of history attracts few real believers.

Alternatively, President Obama may know the details of what he intends, but is not providing them to the public. But if it is necessary to conceal a plan's details to put the best possible public face on it, those details must be adverse.

Claiming adherence to elevated principles, but keeping detailed proposals from sight, also has strategic advantages. You can repeatedly preen as principled, criticizing opponents who offer specifics, without offering any targets for return fire. Any criticism can be parried by saying, "that was not in our proposal" or "we have no plans to do that" or other rhetorical devices. It also allows someone to selectively incorporate others' reform ideas as if they were his idea all along.

The Obama administration, with a long record of vague proposals, has outdone itself by offering virtually nothing concrete in the debt-ceiling negotiations. However, adequate policy cannot rest upon such gossamer foundations. That requires the nuts and bolts so glaringly missing from the White House. Americans wouldn't spend their own money on such amorphous promises of unseen products. They would be foolhardy to treat political sales jobs any differently.

While offering vagueness may be good election strategy, it virtually ensures bad policy, if Americans' welfare is the criterion.

President Barack Obama's conduct during the debate

over the debt ceiling has divided the country and will inflict damage that will last well after the battle is over.

While I believe a debt ceiling deal will get done, I also feel that Obama's behavior has been "unpresidential."

He is dividing us as a nation. He is not bringing us together. He is willfully dividing us. He is petulant!

It distresses me to see what has happened to this country and to know it need not have happened, and to know it has happened because of policies implemented and advanced by someone who is either clueless...or is a saboteur.

Regardless of which he might be, this nation is crumbling on Obama's watch.

In a nostalgic look-back, I can still recall the days of poking fun at Jimmy Carter's follies. But now days, it gets harder and harder to laugh at the things this administration is fumbling day after day.

Under Obama, people's lives are being destroyed. People know that their futures are being cut out from underneath them. In its entire history our country has never been anywhere near the risk it's at today. At no time in the past was it accurate to say "four more years of President X" and this country, as we've known it, will cease to exist. That is today's reality. Four more years of an unchecked, unstopped Obama, and America, as we've known it, will be transformed in ways that we have no desire to see.

I digress, but again...I ask myself, who is this man? I just don't believe he's one of us, and by one of us...I mean a true American with America's best interest as his top priority. He always has that look of arrogances and superiority, his nose up in the air even as he's looking down on the peasants with distain. And his patented, how dare you question my authority, stare down glare. I just don't think he likes us common white folks.

A Coil of Rage:

The character of any man is defined by how he treats his mother as the years pass and need I say more about this person below...other than there is no character, no integrity, but a ton of attitude and arrogance that defines his shallow past and hollow future.

I found his book, Audacity of Hope, to be difficult and disturbing to read considering his attitude toward us and everything American. Allow me to introduce a few phrases he uses (in the book) to describe his attitude toward whites. He harbors a "COIL OF RAGE"...his words, not mine.

Dreams From My Father:

➢ "I ceased to advertise my mother's race at the age of 12 or 13, when I began to suspect that by doing so I was ingratiating myself to whites."

➢ "I found a solace in nursing a pervasive sense of grievance and animosity against my mother's race."

➢ "There was something about her that made me wary, a little too sure of herself, maybe and white."

➢ "It remained necessary to prove which side you were on, to show your loyalty to the black masses, to strike out and name names."

➢ "I never emulate white men and brown men whose fates didn't speak to my own. It was into my father's image, the black man, son of Africa, that I had packed all the attributes I sought in myself: the attributes of Martin and Malcolm, DuBois and Mandela."

Audacity of Hope:

> "I will stand with the Muslims should the political winds shift in an ugly direction."

In the statement about, the word "Muslims" was an inference to Arab and Pakistani immigrants who expressed their concerns (after 9/11) regarding another Japanese-like interment camps situation...should Islamic terrorists attacked America again.

Snopes: "Mostly True"

Just so we all understand, the current administration did not bring us to the brink...our slide has been gaining momentum for decades. But "he" is the catalyst to push us on over the precipice.

Real time up-date on the debt ceiling negotiations:

The outline that emerged Sunday (July 31, 2011), of a last minute deal to raise the debt ceiling and cut federal spending...disappointed budget experts, who feared that the agreement was politically expedient but appeared to fall far short of serious changes to the big drivers of government spending.

"If that's all they can say, after 12 weeks of intense wrangling, charges and counter-charges, if all they could pass was the basic debt limit, we're very disappointed," said Steve Bell, a senior director at the Bipartisan Policy Center, a think tank comprising former Democratic and Republican power brokers that last year offered an exhaustive plan to tackle the nation's fiscal problems.

What irked Bell and other budget experts was that the plan emerging from congressional and White House officials appeared to take off the table serious attempts to address military spending or changes to Social Security, Medicare and Medicaid.

Most of the cuts agreed on during three-way negotiations among the White House and Senate leaders from each political party were in discretionary spending. They agreed to make steep cuts over 10 years to "a segment of the budget that accounts for less than one-fifth of federal spending."

Of course we already know and understand "wiggle words" like "discretionary," and we're well acquainted with subjective terms like "steep cuts."

We also know that long-term spending cuts often...somehow, get lost in "business as usual."

And one more thing, "reaching a deal" is far from coming up with a solution. Obama just kept prodding the two parties to compromise...compromise! Well, I would suggest that compromising is what brought us, and our country, so far down this dead-end road. We have "compromised" our values, our self-worth, our identity, our children's future, our Christian beliefs, and America... along with our way of life, as we knew it.

And so it is, once again...business as usual. "For people that bragged about not doing business as usual, it is business as usual."

As a dog returns to its vomit, so fools return to their follies.

Just keep kicking that can down the road until it becomes someone else's Waterloo.

The can that Congress keeps kicking down the road is a security blanket for the Democrats and a dilemma for Republicans, the welfare and prerogative programs. The beneficiaries of those various entitlements constitute a hefty voting block capable of making...or breaking, even a career politician.

To paraphrase Shakespeare's "Macbeth" on the debt ceiling resolution: "They are poor players who strut and fret their hour upon the stage and then are heard no more. Theirs is a tale told by idiots full of sound and fury...but signifying nothing else."

The fact of the matter is that there's a refusal on both the Democratic and the Republican side of the aisle to acknowledge the mathematical problem that America has, which is that the United States is being bled dry by an entirely integrated system of extractions: financial system, trading system, taxing system, welfare and entitlement systems, sponsorship system, aid to other countries system, and every other imaginable give-a-way system...and it was created by both parties over a period of decades. And now we're sitting here arguing about whether we should do the $4 trillion plan that kicks the can down the road for the next president or burn the place to the ground, both of which are reckless, irresponsible and stupid.

Debt ceiling history quiz:

"The fact that we are here today to debate raising America's debt limit is a sign of leadership failure. It is a sign that the U.S. Government can't pay its own bills. It is a sign that we now depend on ongoing financial assistance from foreign countries to finance our government's reckless fiscal policies.

Increasing America's debt weakens us domestically and

internationally. Leadership means that 'the buck stops here.' Instead, Washington is shifting the burden of bad choices today onto the backs of our children and grand-children. America has a debt problem and a failure of leadership. Americans deserve better."

If you guessed Senator Barack Obama, circa 2006, you would be right.

So once again, Congress ignores Alexander Tyler's truism (1787): "A democracy will continue to exist up until the time that voters discover that they can vote themselves generous gifts from the public treasury."

CHAPTER 29

Most of us older folks can remember the series of "Planet of the Apes" movies. In looking back today, I realize they weren't just about talking apes...they were metaphors. Science running amok, an underclass shrugging off its chains, and how humans treat beings that are lower on the evolutionary scale.

When the first Planet of the Apes movie was released in 1968, the shock of seeing apes on horseback, and that famous Statue of Liberty ending, helped make the film a box-office hit and an instant classic. More than 40 years later, Planet of the Apes has been the subject of numerous parodies and dialogue that has become embedded in the public consciousness.

Those apes mirrored us...in an un-flattering way; they had an extreme class structure, religious dogmatism and military paranoia.

With today's perspective, I can see them as timeless mythology, parables of revolutions from within, fostered by ideology, not an alien or ape invasion. They reflect today's truism that with politicians (I know, scientists were the problem in the movies) there is always the danger of falling short of one's intentions, and individual hubris creating events and side effects that can be our undoing.

Ultimately, all the "Apes" movies have been based on an unchanging set of ideas regarding mankind's innate nature to seek control of his environment. I would suggest that what's really at the core of this hypothesis... is mankind's arrogance. And unfortunately, from day one...that premise hasn't changed. Our arrogance ("perceived invulnerability") makes us extremely "vulnerable" to the arrogance of those who would aspire to control our lives...whether by terrorism, unregulated immigration or "social engineering."

Back in Chapter 23, I presented my vague, cursory opinion of Obama's rapid rise from obscurity to the pinnacle of worldwide success. But there is yet another line of thought/logic/fodder out there...or just another radical right-wing conspiracy theory if you're a liberal/progressive.

If you have ever wondered where Obama came from and just how he so quickly moved from anonymity to President, or why the media is "selective" in what we are told, here is the man who most probably put him there and is responsible. He controls President Obama's every move.

But first, a few defining points for your consideration:

Obama is a very intellectual, charming individual. He is not to be underestimated.

He is a cool customer who doesn't show his emotions. It's very hard to know what's behind the mask. The taking down of the Clinton dynasty was an amazing accomplishment. The Clintons still do not understand what hit them. Obama was in the perfect place at the perfect time.

Obama has political skills comparable to Reagan and Clinton. He has a way of making you think he's on your side, agreeing with your position, while doing the opposite. Pay no attention to what he says; watch what he does!

Obama has a ruthless quest for power. He did not come to Washington to make something out of himself, but rather to change everything, including dismantling capitalism. He can't be straightforward about his ambitions, as the public would not go along. He has a heavy hand, and wants to level the playing field with income redistribution and punishment to the achievers of society. He would like to model the USA to Great Britain or Canada.

His three main goals are to control energy, public education, and national healthcare by having the Federal government run them. He doesn't care about the auto or financial services industries, but got them as an early bonus. The cap and trade will add costs to everything and stifle growth. Paying for "free" college education is also his goal. Most scary is his healthcare program, because if you make it "free" and add 46,000,000 people to a Medicare-type single-payer system, the costs will go through the roof. The only way to control costs is with massive "rationing" of services, like in Canada. God forbid!

He has surrounded himself with mostly far-left academic types. No one around him has ever even run a candy store. But they are going to try and run the auto, financial, banking and other industries. This obviously can't work in the long run. Obama is not a socialist; rather he's a far-left secular progressive bent on nothing short of revolution. He ran as a moderate, but will govern from the hard left. Again, watch what he does, not what he says.

Obama doesn't really see himself as President of the United States, but more as a ruler over the world. He sees himself above it all, trying to orchestrate and coordinate various countries and their agendas. He sees moral equivalency in all cultures. His apology tour to Germany and England was a prime example of how he sees America; as an imperialist nation that has been arrogant, rather than a great noble nation that has at times made errors. This is the first President ever who has chastised our allies and appeased our enemies.

He is now handing out the goodies, while hoping the bill (and pain) will not come due until after he is reelected in 2012. He would like to blame all problems on Bush from the past, and hopefully his successor in the future. He has a huge ego, and I believe he is a narcissist.

The current level of spending is irresponsible and outrageous. We are spending trillions that we don't have. This could lead to hyperinflation, depression or worse. No country has ever spent themselves into prosperity. The media is giving Obama, Reid and Pelosi a pass because they love their agenda. But eventually the bill will come due and people will realize the huge bailouts didn't work, nor will the stimulus package.

These were trillion-dollar payoffs to Obama's allies, unions and the Congress to placate the left, so he could get support for his Obamacare.

But the question still lingers, who is Obama? Obama is a puppet and here is the explanation of the man or demon that pulls his strings. It's not by chance that Obama can manipulate the world. After reading this and Obama's reluctance to accept help on the oil spill you wonder if the spill was part of the plan to destroy the US? "In history, nothing happens by accident; if it happened, you can bet someone planned it," Franklin Delano Roosevelt.

Who Is George Soros? Here is what CBS' Mr. Steve Kroft's research turned up. It's a bit of a read, and it took 4 months to put it together, but we're just going to touch on the areas of relevance to our subject matter:

And yes, this is the same George Soros who was introduced in Chapter 25. My aim is to provide you with enough information that you can understand how one man, with unlimited resources can influence…and even change, the itinerary of nations.

"The main obstacle to a stable and just world order is the United States." George Soros

He has been known to bring down world markets in just days.

George Soros is an evil man. He's anti-God, anti-family, anti-American, anti-Israel and anti-good. What we have in Soros, is a multi-billionaire atheist, with skewed moral values, and a sociopath's lack of conscience. He considers himself to be an elitist world-class philosopher, despises the American way, and just loves to do "social engineering" and change cultures.

In a recent article, Joshua Muravchik describes how Soros has admitted to having carried some rather potent messianic fantasies with him from childhood, which he felt he had to control, otherwise they might get him in trouble. Be that as it may. After WW II, Soros attended the London School of Economics, where he fell under the thrall of fellow atheist and Hungarian, Karl Popper, one of his professors. Popper was a mentor to Soros until Popper's death in 1994. Two of Popper's most influential teachings concerned "the open society," and fallibilism.

Fallibilism is the philosophical doctrine that all claims of knowledge could, in principle, be mistaken. The open society basically refers to a "test and evaluate" approach to social engineering. Regarding open society, Roy Childs writes, "Since the Second World War, most of the Western democracies have followed Popper's advice about piecemeal social engineering and democratic social reform, and it has gotten them into a grand mess."

It was in London that he began thinking deeply about the concept of open societies. He has since been quoted as saying, "Fascism and communism have a lot in common and both stand in opposition to a different principle of social organization, the principle of Open Society."

In 1956 Soros moved toNew York City, where he worked on Wall Street and started amassing his fortune. He specialized in hedge funds and currency speculation. Soros is absolutely ruthless, amoral and clever in his business dealings and quickly made his fortune. By the 1980's he was well on his way to becoming the global powerhouse that he is today.

In an article Kyle-Anne Shiver wrote for The American Thinker, she says, "Soros made his first billion in 1992 by shorting the British pound with leveraged billions in financial bets, and became known as the man who broke the Bank of England. He broke it on the backs of hard-working British citizens who immediately saw their homes severely devalued and their life savings cut drastically, almost overnight."

In 1994 Soros crowed in The New Republic, that "the former Soviet Empire is now called the Soros Empire." The Russia-gate scandal in 1999, which almost collapsed the Russian economy, was labeled by Representative Jim Leach, then head of the House Banking Committee, to be "one of the greatest social robberies in human history." In 1997 Soros almost destroyed the economies of Thailand and Malaysia. At the time Malaysia's Prime Minister, Mahathir Mohammad, called Soros "a villain, and a moron." Thai activist Weng Tojirakarn said, "We regard George Soros as a kind of Dracula. He sucks the blood from the people."

The website Greek National Pride reports, "Soros was part of the full court press that dismantled Yugoslavia and caused trouble in Georgia, Ukraine and Myanmar (Burma). Calling himself a philanthropist, Soros' role is to tighten the ideological stranglehold of globalization and the New World Order while promoting his own financial gain. He is without conscience; a capitalist who functions with absolute amorality."

France has upheld an earlier conviction against Soros for felony insider trading. Soros was fined 2.9 million dollars. Recently, his native Hungary fined Soros 2.2 million dollars for "illegal market manipulation." Elizabeth Crum writes that the Hungarian economy has been in a state of transition as the country seeks to become more financially stable and westernized. By deliberately driving down the share price of its largest bank, Soros put Hungary's economy into a wicked tailspin, one from which it is still trying to recover.

My point here is that Soros is a planetary parasite. His grasp, greed, and gluttony have a global reach. But what about America? Soros told Australia's national newspaper, The Australian, "America, as the center of the globalized financial markets, was sucking up the savings of the world. This is now over. The game is out," he said, adding that the time has come for a very serious adjustment in Americans' consumption habits. He implied that he was the one with the power to bring this about.

"World financial crisis is stimulating and in a way, the culmination of my life's work." George Soros

Soros has been actively working to destroy America from the inside out for some years now. People have been warning us. Two years ago, news sources reported that Soros is an extremist who wants open borders, a one-world foreign policy, legalized drugs, euthanasia, and on and on. This is off the chart dangerous. In 1997 Rachel Ehrenfeld wrote, "Soros uses his philanthropy to change, or more accurately deconstruct, the moral values and attitudes of the Western world and particularly of the American people. His open society is not about freedom; it is about license. His vision rejects the notion of ordered liberty, in favor of a progressive ideology of rights and entitlements."

Perhaps the most important of these "whistle blowers" are David Horowitz and Richard Poe. Their book The Shadow Party outlines in detail how Soros hijacked the Democratic Party, and now owns it lock, stock, and barrel. Soros has been packing the Democratic Party with radicals, and ousting moderate Democrats for years. The Shadow Party became the Shadow Government, which recently became the Obama Administration.

DiscoverTheNetworks.org writes: By his own admission, Soros helped engineer coups in Slovakia, Croatia, Georgia and Yugoslavia. When Soros targets a country for regime change, he begins by creating a shadow government, a fully formed government-in-exile, ready to assume power when the opportunity arises. The Shadow Party he built in America greatly resembled those he created in other countries prior to instigating a coup.

The November 2008 edition of the German magazine Der Spiegel, in which Soros gave his opinion on what the next President of the United States should do after taking office. "I think they need a large stimulus package." Soros thought that around 600 billion dollars would be about right. Soros also said that, "I think Obama presents us with a great opportunity to finally deal with global warming and energy dependence. The United States needs a cap and trade system with auctioning of licenses for emissions rights."

Although Soros doesn't (yet) own the Republican Party, like he does the Democrats, make no mistake; his tentacles are spread throughout the Republican Party as well.

In 2008, Soros donated $5,000,000,000 (that's five billion) to the Democratic National Committee, DNC, to ensure Obama's win and wins for many other Alinsky trained Radical Rules and Anti-American Socialists. George has been contributing billions to the DNC since the Clintons came on the scene.

Soros has dirtied both sides of the aisle, trust me. And if that weren't bad enough, he has long held connections with the CIA. And I mustn't forget to mention Soros' involvement with the MSM (Main Stream Media), the entertainment industry (he owns 2.6 million shares of Time Warner), and the various political advertising organizations he funnels millions to. In short, George Soros controls or influences most of the MSM. Little wonder they ignore the TEA PARTY, Soro's nemesis. As Matthew Vadum writes, "The liberal billionaire-turned-philanthropist has been buying up media properties for years in order to drive home his message to the American public that they are too materialistic, too wasteful, too selfish, and too stupid to decide for themselves how to run their own lives."

Richard Poe writes, "Soros' private philanthropy, totaling untold billions, continues undermining America's traditional Western values. His giving has provided funding for abortion rights, atheism, drug legalization, sex education, euthanasia, feminism, gun control, globalization, mass immigration, gay marriage and other radical experiments in social engineering."

Some of the many NGOs (Non-Government Organizations) that Soros funds with his billions are: MoveOn.org, the Apollo Alliance, Media Matters for America, the Tides Foundation, the ACLU, ACORN, PDIA (Project on Death In America), La Raza, and many more.

Poe continues, "Through his global web of Open Society Institutes and Open Society Foundations, Soros has spent 25 years recruiting, training, indoctrinating and installing a network of loyal operatives in 50 countries, placing them in positions of influence and power in media, government, finance and academia."

Without Soros' money, would Saul Alinsky's Chicago machine still be rolling? Would SEIU, ACORN and La Raza still be pursuing their nefarious activities? Would Big Money and lobbyists still be corrupting government? Would our college campuses still be retirement homes for 1960s radicals?

America stands at the brink of an abyss, and that fact is directly attributable to Soros. Soros has vigorously, cleverly and insidiously planned the ruination of America and his puppet, Barack Obama, is leading the way.

On the eve of the American Revolution in 1776, Tom Paine said, "If there must be trouble, let it be in my day, that my children may have peace."

CHAPTER 30

I t would seem that Obama started life off on the wrong foot; first by not being comfortable with the color of his mother's skin and then spending most of his adult life associating with anti-America and anti-capitalism radicals intent on destroying America and everything it stands for.

As a Community Organizer he found his calling in the black ghettos of Chicago where he bonded with Bill Ayers and Pastor Jeremiah Wright while embracing Saul Alinsky's book entitled: "Rules for Radicals"

I am aware, and have been for some time of the Obama and Saul Alinsky connection, the Alinsky plan, and how his star pupil, now in the White House, is enacting it. But this piece puts a fine point on it and, with the benefit of two and a half years of history behind us, the reality of it should be screaming to all of us, "Wake up America... before it's too late!"

As a disciple of Alinsky's book and training, Obama is using Rules for Radicals as a manual for his "Social engineering agenda."

President Obama is fond of using ridicule to frustrate critics. He recently mocked Republicans for predicting "Armageddon" if health care reform passed. After signing the bill, he cracked that he looked around to see if there were any asteroids falling, only to discover a nice day with birds chirping.

Obama has also used the tactic to dismiss charges that he's pushing a "socialist" agenda, arguing that critics will next accuse him of "being a secret communist because I shared my toys in kindergarten."

But the former community organizer also knows that ridiculing the opposition is an effective tactic taught by the father of community organizing, Saul D. Alinsky...a socialist agitator from Chicago whose influence on Obama is deeper than commonly known.

In fact, the tactic is ripped right from the pages of Rules for Radicals (Vintage Books, New York, 1971), a how-to manual Alinsky wrote for coat-and-tie revolutionaries.

"Ridicule is man's most potent weapon," reads Rule No. 5. "It is almost impossible to counterattack ridicule. Also it infuriates the opposition, who then react to your advantage."

It's just one of 11 rules Alinsky coached his acolytes to follow to "take power away from the Haves." The Haves, represented foremost by corporate America, are "the enemy." They must be identified, singled out and targeted for attack...and the more personal the better, Alinsky advised, putting a special bull's-eye on banks.

His 11th rule..."Pick the target, freeze it, personalize it and polarize it"...is not lost on Obama, who has targeted "fat cat" bankers, "predatory" lenders, "greedy" insurers and industrial "polluters" as enemies of the people.

"Obama learned his lesson well," said David Alinsky, son of the late socialist. "I am proud to see that my father's model for organizing is being applied successfully beyond local community organizing."

"True revolutionaries do not flaunt their radicalism," Alinsky taught. "They cut their hair, put on suits and infiltrate the system from within." Alinsky viewed revolution as a slow, patient process. The trick is to penetrate existing institutions such as churches, unions and political parties. Many leftists view Hillary as a sell-out because she claims to hold moderate views on some issues. However, Hillary is simply following Alinsky's counsel to do and say whatever it takes to gain power.

Obama is also an Alinskyite. He spent years teaching workshops on the Alinsky method. In 1985 he began a four-year stint as a community organizer in Chicago, working for an Alinskyite group called the Developing Communities Project. Camouflage is the key to Alinsky-style organizing. While trying to build coalitions of black churches in Chicago, Obama caught flak for not attending church himself. He then became an instant church-goer...at Pastor Jeremiah Wright's Trinity United Church of Christ.

Their relationship would span two decades before Obama would be forced to distance himself from Wright, as he became a liability to Obama's aspirations. During those years, Wright officiated at the wedding ceremony of Barack and Michelle Obama, as well as their children's baptisms.

Yes, the same Pastor Wright who proclaimed, "God damn America for treating our citizens as less than human. God damn America for as long as she acts like she is God and she is supreme." In addition to damning America, he told his congregation on the Sunday after September

11, 2001, that the United States had brought on Qaeda's attacks because of its own terrorism.

Note: "Gamaliel" is a network of organizers working "tirelessly" behind the scenes to train community leaders.

They helped him get into Harvard Law School to "learn about power's currency in all its intricacy and detail," as Obama put it in his memoir. A Gamaliel board member even wrote a letter of recommendation for him.

Obama later took a break from his Harvard studies to travel to Los Angeles for eight days of intense training at the Alinsky Industrial Areas Foundation. In turn, he trained other community organizers in Alinsky agitation tactics. In 1988, he even wrote an additional chapter for the book "After Alinsky: Community Organizing in Illinois," in which he lamented organizers' "lack of power" in implementing change.

Decades later, power would no longer be an issue, as Obama infiltrated the highest echelons of the political establishment, thus fulfilling Alinsky's vision of a new "vanguard" of coat-and-tie radicals sneaking in behind enemy lines. He preached that changing the system "means working within the system"...while not acting or looking radical. "Start them easy," he said in his book, "don't scare them too soon."

It worked like a charm for Obama. And during the presidential campaign, he hired one of his Gamaliel mentors, Mike Kruglik, to train young campaign workers in Alinsky tactics at "Camp Obama," a school set up at Obama headquarters in Chicago. The tactics helped Obama capture the youth vote like no other president before him.

After the election, his other Gamaliel mentor, Jerry Kellman (who actually hired him and whose identity

Obama disguised in his memoir), helped the Obama administration establish Organizing for America, which mobilizes young supporters to agitate for Obama's legislative agenda using Rules for Radicals which Alinsky dedicated to "Lucifer; the very first radical known to man who rebelled against the establishment and did it so effectively that he, at least, won his own kingdom."

In fact, the 1971 book, now selling well on Amazon, is required reading for students applying for the program.

"Rules" is more than a manual. It's a diary of Alinsky's worldview, a dark, anti-capitalist one made all the more disturbing knowing that his protégé sits in the Oval Office, where he's systematically reorganizing our economy, one industry at a time.

A careful reading of Alinsky's 200-page book leaves you queasy. Even before you get to his rules, which start on Page 126, you realize he hates everything dear to Americans while respecting nothing sacred about America...even its founding. He ridicules our most basic morality. He mocks our founders, finding the worst even in Jefferson, a classical liberal.

Alinsky, who died of a heart attack at 63, valued democracy merely as a "means" toward achieving "economic justice." He laughed at "middle-class moral hygiene." He even rebuked activists burdened by decency and troubled by the ethics of his tactics, sneering that they would rather go home with their "ethical hymen intact" than win a battle at any cost.

Alinsky was more than a socialist. He was a moral anarchist. Listen to these perverse proverbs:

➢ "Ethical standards must be elastic."

- ➤ "In war the end justifies almost any means."

- ➤ "In a fight almost anything goes."

- ➤ "It is a world not of angels but of angles."

- ➤ "The real arena is corrupt."

- ➤ "Reconciliation means that when one side gets the power and the other side gets reconciled to it, then we have reconciliation." GOP lawmakers take note.

- ➤ "All values are relative."

Bitterly contemptuous of American materialism and individualism, Alinsky was a big fan of Lenin, whom he called a "pragmatist." He claimed that his own philosophy was anchored in "hope" for a more just world.

But this privileged son was simply bored with the status quo and sought to smash it just to see it smashed, while masquerading his unprincipled pique as an altruistic crusade for the downtrodden.

"Agitate," he egged on fellow radicals, "create disenchantment and discontent with the current values," even if none exist.

His story is similar to that of unrepentant terrorist Bill Ayers, the rebellious son of a successful Chicago businessman. Alinsky's father owned his own business in the city and put his son through the University of Chicago studying archeology.

Alinsky comes across loud and clear in the narrative of Rules for Radicals as a bitter, vulgar Hobbesian cynic. He advocates "fart-ins" and "shit-ins" to offend the establishment, explaining that the "one thing" that inner city organizers want to do to whites is "shit on them." Nothing is off limits. The only thing he truly romanticizes is "ego."

"The ego of the organizer is stronger and more monumental than the ego of the leader," he wrote. "The organizer is in a true sense reaching for the highest level for which man can reach...to play God." He added: "Ego must be so all-pervading that the personality of the organizer is contagious."

According to Alinsky, the organizer, especially a paid organizer from outside...must first overcome suspicion and establish credibility. Next the organizer must begin the task of agitating, rubbing resentments, fanning hostilities, and searching out controversy. This is necessary to get people to participate. An organizer has to attack apathy and disturb the prevailing patterns of complacent community life where people have simply come to accept a situation. Alinsky would say, "The first step in community organization is community disorganization."

Through a process of combining hope and resentment, the organizer tries to create a "mass army" that brings in as many recruits as possible from local organizations, churches, services groups, labor unions, corner gangs, and individuals.

Alinsky provides a collection of rules to guide the process. But he emphasizes these rules must be translated into real-life tactics that are fluid and responsive to the situation at hand.

Rule 1: Power is not only what you have, but what an opponent thinks you have. If your organization is small, hide your numbers in the dark and raise a din that will make everyone think you have many more people than you do.

Rule 2: Never go outside the experience of your people. The result is confusion, fear, and retreat.

Rule 3: Whenever possible, go outside the experience of an opponent. Here you want to cause confusion, fear, and retreat.

Rule 4: Make opponents live up to their own book of rules. "You can kill them with this, for they can no more obey their own rules than the Christian church can live up to Christianity."

Rule 5: Ridicule is man's most potent weapon. It's hard to counterattack ridicule, and it infuriates the opposition, which then reacts to your advantage.

Rule 6: A good tactic is one your people enjoy. "If your people aren't having a ball doing it, there is something very wrong with the tactic."

Rule 7: A tactic that drags on for too long becomes a drag. Commitment may become ritualistic as people turn to other issues.

Rule 8: Keep the pressure on. Use different tactics and actions and use all events of the period for your purpose. "The major premise for tactics is the development of operations that will maintain a constant pressure upon the opposition. It is this that will cause the opposition to react to your advantage."

Rule 9: The threat is more terrifying than the thing itself. When Alinsky leaked word that large numbers of poor people were going to tie up the washrooms of O'Hare Airport, Chicago city authorities quickly agreed to act on a longstanding commitment to a ghetto organization. They imagined the mayhem as thousands of passengers poured off airplanes to discover every washroom occupied. Then they imagined the international embarrassment and the damage to the city's reputation.

Rule 10: The price of a successful attack is a constructive alternative. Avoid being trapped by an opponent or an interviewer who says, "Okay, what would you do?"

Rule 11: Pick the target, freeze it, personalize it, and polarize it. Don't try to attack abstract corporations or bureaucracies. Identify a responsible individual. Ignore attempts to shift or spread the blame.

According to Alinsky, the main job of the organizer is to bait an opponent into reacting. "The enemy properly goaded and guided in his reaction will be your major strength."

Alinsky continues by stating several rules of the ethics of means and ends:

> The judgment of the ethics of means is dependent upon the political position of those sitting in judgment.

> In war, the end justifies almost any means.

> Judgment must be made in the context of the times in which the action occurred and not from any other chronological vantage point.

> Concern with ethics increases with the number of means available and vice versa. The less important the end to be desired, the more one can afford to engage in ethical evaluations of means.

> Generally, success or failure is a mighty determinant of ethics.

> ➢ The morality of a means depends upon whether the means is being employed at a time of imminent defeat or imminent victory.

> ➢ Any effective means is automatically judged by the opposition as being unethical.

> ➢ You do what you can with what you have and clothe it with moral garments. Goals must be phrased in general terms like Liberty, Equality, Fraternity, Of the Common Welfare, Pursuit of Happiness, or Bread and Peace.

Page 23 of Rules is chilling: The American individualist... the industrialist, the entrepreneur, the wealth creator... "is beginning to learn that he will either share part of his material wealth or lose all of it; that he will respect and learn to live with other political ideologies"...that is, neo-Marxism, "if he wants civilization to go on."

"If he does not share his bread, he dare not sleep, for his neighbor will kill him," Alinsky warned. In other words, sacrifice and pay your fair share for "social justice" (code for socialism) or face mass unrest and the anger of the mob. Anarchy. Chaos. Blood in the streets.

Alinsky describes "the Haves" of American society as having fallen asleep...ripe for slaughter. "It is as though the great law of change had prepared the anesthetization of the victim prior to the social surgery to come."

Obama is acting as Alinsky's star social surgeon, the first to possess the necessary power to carve up the American economy for mass redistribution? "Rules for Radicals" is his operating manual...and more of us should be reading it.

Here again, we have the handmaiden scenario, there can be no doubt that George Soros knew exactly what he had found in Obama. Soros had the money and power and Obama had the favorable skin pigmentation, arrogance, inflated ego, animosity toward whites and America...and an innate kinship to the "The Muslim World."

Enough said, you either understand or you're burdened by artificial stupidity.

CHAPTER 30: PART 2

The American Heritage Dictionary's definition of socialism:

Any of various theories or systems of social organization in which the means of producing and distributing goods is owned collectively or by a centralized government that often plans and controls the economy.

In the Marxist-Leninist theory, the intermediate stage between capitalism and communism, in which collective ownership of the economy, under the dictatorship of the proletariat, has not yet been successfully achieved.

Historical fact #1: Socialism has been a stepping-stone for dictators and Communism governments throughout history.

"The Naked Communist" is a book written in 1958 by conservative United States author and faith-based political theorist Cleon Skousen.

The book posits and seeks to describe a geopolitical strategy by which the Marxist-Leninist Soviet Union was attempting to overcome and control all the governments of the world that were not members of the Communist bloc. At the time the book was published, during the Cold War, fear of communism was common among people in non-communist nations.

In 1960, The Church of Jesus Christ of Latter-day Saints president David O. McKay recommended that all members of his church read The Naked Communist.

U.S. Congressman Albert S. Herlong, Jr. of Florida read the list of communist goals, contained in the book, into the Congressional Records, on January 10, 1963.

The Naked Communist and its author enjoyed a resurgence in popularity during the early part of the 21st century, primarily due to attention paid by American radio and conservative political commentator, Glenn Beck. Beck said that The Naked Communist was among the books that "changed my life."

The following is the list of Communist goals contained in The Naked Communist:

1) U.S. acceptance of coexistence as the only alternative to atomic war.

2) U.S. willingness to capitulate in preference to engaging in atomic war.

3) Develop the illusion that total disarmament by the United States would be a demonstration of moral strength.

4) Permit free trade between all nations regardless of Communist affiliation and regardless of whether or not items could be used for war.

5) Extension of long-term loans to Russia and Soviet satellites.

6) Provide American aid to all nations regardless of Communist domination.

7) Grant recognition of Red China. Admission of Red China to the U.N.

8) Set up East and West Germany as separate states in spite of Khrushchev's promise in 1955 to settle the German question by free elections under supervision of the U.N.

9) Prolong the conferences to ban atomic tests because the United States has agreed to suspend tests as long as negotiations are in progress.

10) Allow all Soviet satellites individual representation in the U.N.

11) Promote the U.N. as the only hope for mankind. If its charter is rewritten, demand that it be set up as a one-world government with its own independent armed forces.

12) Resist any attempt to outlaw the Communist Party.

13) Do away with all loyalty oaths (example: our Pledge of Allegiance to The United States).

14) Continue giving Russia access to the U.S. Patent Office.

15) Capture one or both of the political parties in the United States.

16) Use technical decisions of the courts to weaken basic

American institutions by claiming their activities violate civil rights.

17) Get control of the schools. Use them as transmission belts for socialism and current Communist propaganda. Soften the curriculum. Get control of teachers' associations. Put the party line in textbooks.

18) Gain control of all student newspapers.

19) Use student riots to foment public protests against programs or organizations that would undermine Communism.

20) Infiltrate the press. Get control of book-review assignments, editorial writing, and policymaking positions.

21) Gain control of key positions in radio, TV, and motion pictures.

22) Continue discrediting American culture by degrading all forms of artistic expression. Skousen claimed that an American Communist cell was told to "eliminate all good sculpture from parks and buildings, substitute shapeless, awkward and meaningless forms."

23) Control art critics and directors of art museums.

24) Eliminate all laws governing obscenity by calling them "censorship" and a violation of free speech and free press.

25) Break down cultural standards of morality by promoting pornography and obscenity in books, magazines, motion pictures, radio, and TV.

26) Present homosexuality, degeneracy and promiscuity as

"normal, natural, healthy." Skousen claimed Communists sought to encourage the practice of masturbation.

27) Infiltrate the churches and replace revealed religion with "social" religion. Discredit the Bible and emphasize the need for intellectual maturity, which does not need a "religious crutch."

28) Eliminate prayer or any phase of religious expression in the schools on the ground that it violates the principle of "separation of church and state."

29) Discredit the American Constitution by calling it inadequate, old-fashioned, out of step with modern needs, a hindrance to cooperation between nations on a world-wide basis.

30) Discredit the American Founding Fathers. Present them as selfish aristocrats who had no concern for the "common man."

31) Belittle all forms of American culture and discourage the teaching of American history on the ground that it was only a minor part of the "big picture." Give more emphasis to Russian history since the Communists took over.

32) Support any socialist movement to give centralized control over any part of the culture...education, social agencies, welfare programs, mental health clinics, etc.

33) Eliminate all laws or procedures which interfere with the operation of the Communist apparatus.

34) Eliminate the House Committee on Un-American Activities.

35) Discredit and eventually dismantle the FBI.

36) Infiltrate and gain control of more unions.

37) Infiltrate and gain control of big business.

38) Transfer some of the powers of arrest from the police to social agencies. Treat all behavioral problems as psychiatric disorders which no one but psychiatrists can understand or treat.

39) Dominate the psychiatric profession and use mental health laws as a means of gaining coercive control over those who oppose Communist goals.

40) Discredit the family as an institution. Encourage promiscuity, masturbation and easy divorce.

41) Emphasize the need to raise children away from the negative influence of parents. Attribute prejudices, mental blocks and retarding of children to suppressive influence of parents.

42) Create the impression that violence and insurrection are legitimate aspects of the American tradition; that students and special-interest groups should rise up and use "united force" to solve economic, political or social problems.

43) Overthrow all colonial governments before native populations are ready for self-government.

44) Internationalize the Panama Canal.

45) Repeal the Connally reservation so the United States cannot prevent the World Court from seizing jurisdiction over domestic problems. Give the World Court jurisdiction over nations and individuals alike.

I would agree that a couple of the line items are in the

fringe area, but the vast majority are all commonalities and traits found throughout history when dissecting dictatorships. I would also suggest we are already familiar with most of the goals...even as the others, appearing on the horizon...are inching forward as our naive and disbelieving citizenry continues to buy the administration's narrative. Very troubling...

Historical fact #2: "Self-deceit, this fatal weakness of mankind, is the source of half the disorders of human life."

Adam Smith

EPILOGUE

A merica is suffering from a surfeit of liberal dreamers. The growth of liberal/progressive ideas in this
country has been escalating for decades. It reached its
political zenith with the 2008 elections. Even though the
2010 elections somewhat blunted liberal political power,
liberal ideas have now permeated America society to a
point where our ancestors would have a hard time recognizing the country they gave us.

Liberals are dreamers. They have their minds made up,
never mind the facts, history or common sense. Even
though liberal ideology has never worked in the real
world, liberals ignore this inconvenient truth. The truth
is that their philosophy is diametrically opposed to the
tenets of individual freedom and self-reliance.

Liberals see the world through darkly tinted glasses. To
them, it matters not that collectivism has never worked
in large societies. Wealth redistribution, the hallmark
of liberal ideology, goes back over 250 years, well before
Karl Marx. The French philosopher Morelly wrote in his
1755 work, "Code of Nature": "Every citizen will be a
public man, sustained by, supported by and occupied at
the public expense."

This is their core dream, birth-to-death succor by the government, and it is alive and well in today's liberal ideology. To implement these ideals, of course, they need the fruits of other people's labor. As our president said, "I think when you spread the wealth around, it's good for everybody." That those people, whose hard-earned "wealth" is being confiscated to give to others, might not agree doesn't matter.

This is not to say that dreamers, per se, haven't made the world a better place. Men and women pursuing their dreams are responsible for some of the greatest accomplishments in human history...and some of the world's greatest catastrophes. Whatever the dream might be... dreamers are convinced they are right, and everyone else is wrong. This makes them more than willing to tell everyone else what to do.

While President Barack Obama may be the current poster child of liberal dreamers and their best-known spokesman, liberal ideology has been undermining American ideas for much longer than he has been alive. Obama developed his ideology growing up from beliefs that were already present in society. From the New Deal, to the Great Society, to Hope and Change, the liberal mindset has infiltrated education, the mainstream media, and the entertainment industry to such an extent that today these institutions are basically cheerleaders for the liberal movement. This is a big part of why liberal power has grown and the American way of life is in jeopardy.

The reality, however, is that liberal values just don't work. For starters, cradle-to-grave security cannot be provided for everyone when there is not enough money to pay for it. Over the decades, liberal thinking and policies have turned a larger and larger portion of our society into the grasshoppers from Aesop's fables, except in the liberal version the grasshopper is "invited" in to share with the ant. Common sense dictates that this means both the grasshopper and the ant will have half rations. To liberals this is just tough luck for the ant. But the liberals never think to ask, "what will happen if the ants decide to stop working."

We must vote those politicians, who espouse the liberal views that have gotten us into our current sorry state of affairs, out of office. We must elect those who want to cut the size of government, reduce and reform unsustainable entitlements, eliminate inefficient programs, and remove unnecessary rules and regulations that strangle business. If we don't, we are destined for a dismal future.

The economy is on the verge of collapse, markets plummeting all over the globe, the S&P downgrades our credit rating, Wall Street drops another four hundred points, the NASDAQ loses 5 percent, unemployment claims keep growing, financial experts fear we are slipping into a double-dip recession, JPMorgan announces they don't expect the economy to grow much faster over the next twelve months than it did during the first half of this year...stagnant, Europe is in big financial trouble, the Deutsche Bank is in the "red" and Bank of America is laying off employees as it faces bankruptcy here in America, and what is our Profligate-in-Chief's response to all this mess...much of it of his own making? "Michelle, let's take another pricey vacation."

I wonder if Obama will play the violin at Martha's Vineyard, while watching America burn from across the water...but then, Obama was vetted so little by the worshipful Obama-lapping Mainstream Media, that we know practically nothing about the man, not even if he does have any musical talents. We are finding out about our narcissist "Presidential Nero" the hard way.

All we know is that he went to Yale and Harvard, thanks to Affirmative Action and his Communist Mentors, and that he speaks with good diction and not in "Ebonics"...thanks to his "White Devil" grandparents, and that he's black.

Like Nero, who was only slightly less "debaucherous" than Caligula, Obama, with wine on his lips...treats "we the people" the way Caligula treated those over whom he lorded.

It is clear that Obama and family view themselves as royalty, but they're not. They are employees of "we the people," who are suffering because of his failed policies. What message does this behavior send to those who to-day are suffering as never before?

This man campaigned on bringing people together, some-thing he has never, ever done in his professional life. In my assessment, Obama will divide us along philosophi-cal lines, push us apart, and then try to realign the pieces into a new and different power structure. Change is indeed coming. And when it comes, you will never see the same nation again.

Many in America wanted to be proud when the first person of color was elected president, but instead, they have been witness to a congenital liar, a woman who has been ashamed of America her entire life, failed policies, intimidation and a commonality hitherto not witnessed in our political leaders. He and his wife view their life, at our expense, as an entitlement...while America's people go homeless, hungry and unemployed.

The liberals' dream will become America's nightmare.

And make no mistake, there will always be another Obama "type" waiting in the wings to take the hand-off and run with Socialism's baton.

FROM THE BALCONY

B ecause this book is being written in real time a lot of my concerns, observations and conjectures will not be validated, or debunked...until long after this book is published. The answers, like the book, will only materialize in real time, but unlike the book today...the answers are down the road.

So with that said, I will use this chapter to personalize a few of my concerns, observations and conjectures regarding America today:

I must acknowledge that life is always evolving but it's such a stealth-like process that it goes unnoticed until one no longer recognizes their surroundings. It happens over a lifetime, in very small incremental phases... but always pervasive and I'm sure, worldwide. I'm also sure that the continuing growth and prosperity of our country was originally viewed as progress, but at some point in time...now lost in history, progress progressed to "Progressivism."

Recently while on one of my road trips, I, for whatever reason...began noticing things that I hadn't been aware of before. These were not things that weren't there last month or even last year; but they are (for the most part) things that have been evolving and accumulating over the years. I would suggest that the driver for our ever-changing landscape is the escalating number of en-croaching immigrates.

I felt as though I was an observer from another dimen-sion or a parallel universe. I can't say why, but up until then...I hadn't really become aware of how dramatically my country's demographics had changed...and are con-tinuing to change. While driving through America, I'm observing signage that I can't read...because I only speak and read English. And everywhere I go today, America seems to be in various stages of decay.

Rural America now accounts for just 16 percent of the nation's population, the lowest ever.

The latest 2010 census numbers hint at an emerging America where, by mid-century, city boundaries will be-come indistinct and rural areas will grow even less rel-evant. Many communities could shrink to virtual ghost towns as they shutter businesses and close down schools, demographers say.

More metro areas are booming into sprawling megalopo-lises. But barring fresh investment that could bring jobs, large swaths of the Great Plains and Appalachia, along with parts of Arkansas, Mississippi and north Texas, could face significant population declines.

These places posted some of the biggest losses over the past decade as young adults left and the people who stayed got older, past childbearing years.

Some of the most isolated rural areas face a major uphill battle, with broad areas of the country emptying out. Many rural areas can't attract workers because there aren't any jobs, and businesses won't relocate there because there aren't enough qualified workers. So they are caught in a downward death spiral.

Delta Air Lines recently announced it would end flight service to 24 small airports; several of them in the Great Plains, and the U.S. Postal Service is mulling plans to close thousands of branches in mostly rural areas of the country.

While rural America shrinks, larger U.S. metropolitan areas have enjoyed double-digit percentage gains in population over the past several decades. Since 2000, metros grew overall by 11 percent with the biggest gains in suburbs or small to medium-sized cities.

My thoughts around the above paragraphs are that rural America has always been home to patriotic Christians. I fear that with the declining nature of rural America, and the growing influence of multicultural metropolitan areas, we're seeing the fading vestige of what once defined who we were...and what we stood for.

We seem to have become a more agitated and combative world with hateful, mean-spirited, anonymous bloggers, and on-line social networking sites where anything goes... even airing out dirty laundry. These mindless tell-all people are tied to their make believe world and can't disconnect because their self-worth depends on their virtual friends' approval...the real world is too much for them.

We have also become a country of protesters; we're seeing more and more protesting that becomes physical and ugly. A growing indicator of how divided America has become.

Posturing has become a troubling, cultural trait amongst many young men today. We are too quick to react, and too slow to apologize.

A routine interpretation of the phrase "survival of the fittest" would seem to mean that "only the fittest organisms will prevail" (a view sometimes derided as Social Darwinism), which is not consistent with the actual theory of evolution.

Darwin first used the phrase "survival of the fittest" as a synonym for natural selection in the fifth edition of his "On the Origin of Species," published in 1869. Darwin meant it as a metaphor for "better adapted for immediate, local environment," not the common inference of "in the best physical shape." Hence, it is not a scientific description.

I always took the term literally and tried to live a healthy life while working hard to be self-sustaining. I've never lived at the expense of others (government) or expected anyone...other than myself, to support my existence.

Darwin must have been a forward-looking man in that he somehow foresaw our welfare state (pun intended). As he suggested, survival is about adaptability to one's immediate and local environment. Generations of welfare recipients have survived just fine, thank you...by adapting. And in looking around, we can quickly ascertain that fitness has had nothing to do with their survival.

The down side to their survival is that while they maintain a physical existence, they pay a high emotional, psychological and self-worth price. I have to wonder if the system doesn't just produce an endless flow of culturally crippled and ethically depleted individuals. A wasteland of humanity...

Of course the road to welfare was paved with good intentions, but with hindsight, we can now see that those good intentions morphed into an all-consuming sub-culture... supported by our government.

I would place most of the blame on our government for continuing to support a system that requires so little from the beneficiaries. I also believe the government's minimum wage program pushed many low-end employees out of the job market, instead of allowing the free market system to level the employment field accordingly.

Young people today (generally speaking) will not bend over to pick up a coin from the ground or bother recycling cans and bottles that they or their parents paid a deposit on, but they have no qualms about going to their parents for money, who are often strapped themselves. I feel, for a number of reasons...that our younger generations are losing their way in today's speeded-up, entitlement world.

While I'm on my soapbox about our younger generation(s), I've often made reference to their lack of perspective regarding yesteryear, as a negative. But there are upsides to be found even in negatives...one just has to look a little harder sometime. Without yesteryears' old school perspective, they are being spared the moaning of those losses that my generation is currently experiencing.

We've all seen the recent rioting across Europe as socialist countries are beginning to crack and tumble like dominos. They're running out of "other people's money" and the entitlements and freebies are evaporating.

"And they thought those days would never end."

But the bigger question is, will Americans riot when America hits that same wall?

First, no one will continue selling a product after the profit has been taken out. Those in the private sector will not support losing propositions. Second, when taxes are raised, and items cost more, people will change their behavior. Those in the private sector make choices about items depending on their cost. Liberals in our government do not behave the way the rest of us do. Therefore, they do not understand the above points.

European politicians have recently backed away from some socialist policies because they see that the above two propositions are true, and that socialism doesn't work. There is only enough money for the socialist elites. Yet many European citizens still believe socialism works and are rioting because the "free stuff" is no longer available.

What do Americans understand? Do they understand the above? Do they remember the gas lines when Jimmy Carter imposed price controls? Many are aghast when they see a big number associated with an oil company's profits, but do not notice when an even bigger number represents congressional spending.

Government's rationale is "always" the same..."necessity." One could argue that necessity has been the argument for every impingement of human freedom; it is the argument of tyrants and the creed of slaves.

We all saw the aftermath of Japan's disastrous tsunami that followed a major earthquake earlier this year. I think most of us were impressed by the people of Japan, we didn't see a culture of individual entitlements. Everyone worked together, there was no looting or civil unrest... they came together as a people, for the common good of the whole. Later when the lines starting forming for gasoline, water and food...they were organized, orderly and without any "me first" mentality disrupting the process. And later when older men (because they had already lived a good long life) volunteered to work in the areas of the radioactive contamination; they were willing to give their lives for the survival of their culture, their country and ultimately...once again, for the whole.

There was once a time in America (long ago) where perhaps we could have emulated Japan, but I fear that today the populace would rip America apart with its divided loyalties and selfishness. We have misplaced our founding fathers' values, our identity, our character, our love of country and we have forsaken God. But additionally we have lost that "wholeness" that brought the Japanese through their recent crisis. We've lost that intangible because we no longer know (from <u>top</u> to <u>bottom</u>) who's standing beside, behind, or with us...we are no longer a whole people. Our country has been ripped apart by political correctness and self-serving and/or spineless politicians.

Having spent my working years in the oil industry, I learned that every breakdown (of our operating equipment) had a "root cause" that precipitated the failure. In order to better understand the causal factor(s), a "Root Cause Failure Analysis" would be facilitated to understand and perhaps prevent a reoccurrence.

But "we" have waited too long to perform such an analysis because our failures have been mounting until the root cause is lost in the wreckage. If America's obituary should ever be written, the cause of "Her" demise would be a long list of contributing factors:

> ➢ Career politicians.

> ➢ The erosion of old school values and work ethic.

> ➢ The always-growing entitlement mentality.

> ➢ The woe is me, victim mentality, joining the entitlement parade.

> ➢ Progressivism's stealth like encroachments into every facet of our lives...even pushing its progressive

educational ideologies in our government run schools, while encouraging the above mentalities... which has promoted government dependency.

➤ Real parenting has fallen by the wayside...allowing government even more and more intrusion into our everyday lives.

➤ Then along came "Political Correctness," to make us all nicer to each other...and if you're buying that line of crap, you're either a progressive/liberal or you've been living in a cave.

➤ Capitalism is currently on life-support.

➤ And then...to add insult to injury, we've slowly... but steadily been moving away from our Christian foundation...turning our backs to God.

➤ But it got worse: The messiah came to us, from out of nowhere...to lead the lost to the Promised Land, "A New World Order."

We hear a lot about tolerance...and being tolerant these today, but interestingly...it's usually in the context of something to do with Islam and/or ethnicity. But on the other hand, it seems there's an ever-growing intolerance toward Christianity. Could it be an intimidation thing? We've heard about some pretty outrageous things (from threats of mayhem to actually killing offenders) happening to individuals and groups who dared to challenge and/or question the Islam religion...and God forbid you ridicule or make a joke at its expense.

But those forgiving Christians; blasphemy, ridicule, name-calling...sticks and stone may break their bones (Oh wait, that's a Muslim thing.), but words will never hurt them. Their retaliation will be more along the lines of something like this: "Bless your heart my friend, you're entitled to your opinion...misguided as it is, but I will pray that you find understanding before it's too late. God bless you."

Could it be because Christians are not very intimidating, that tolerance for them is non-existent?

And of course, the liberal/progressive community would just as soon see the Christian community disappear into the next sunset.

Here's a modest proposal for liberals who say they support job creation: Stop smearing successful, law-abiding private companies whose values don't comport with yours. I'm looking at you, New York Times.

Chick-fil-A is an American success story. Founded by Georgian entrepreneur Truett Cathy in 1946, the family-owned chicken-sandwich chain is one of the country's largest fast-food businesses. It employs some 50,000 workers across the country at 1,500 outlets in nearly 40 states and the District of Columbia. The company generates more than $2 billion in revenue and serves millions of happy customers with trademark Southern hospitality.

So, what's the problem? Well, devout Christians who believe in strong marriages, devoted families, and the highest standards of character for their workers run Chick-fil-A. The restaurant chain's official corporate mission is to "glorify God" and "enrich the lives of everyone we touch." The company's community-service initiatives, funded through its WinShape Foundation, support foster-care, scholarship, summer-camp, and marriage-enrichment programs. On Sunday, all Chick-fil-A stores close so workers can spend the day at worship and rest.

For the Left, these Biblically based corporate principles constitute social-justice high crimes and misdemeanors.

Democrats are always ready to invoke religion to support their big-government, taxpayer-funded initiatives (Obamacare, illegal-alien amnesty, increased education spending, and FCC regulatory expansion, for starters). But when an independent company...thriving on its own merits in the marketplace, wears its soul on its sleeve, suddenly it's a theocratic crisis.

Over the past month, several progressive-activist blogs have waged an ugly war against Chick-fil-A. The company's alleged atrocity; one of its independent outlets in Pennsylvania donated some sandwiches and brownies to a marriage seminar run by the Pennsylvania Family Institute, which happens to oppose same-sex marriage.

In the name of tolerance, the anti-Chick-fil-A hawks sneered at the company's main product as "Jesus Chicken," derided its no-Sunday-work policy, and attacked its operators as "anti-gay." Michael Jones, who describes himself as having "worked in the field of human rights communications for a decade, most recently for Harvard Law School," launched an online petition drive at www.change.org "demanding" that the company disavow "extreme anti-gay groups." Facebook users dutifully organized witch hunts against the company on college campuses.

Over the weekend, New York Times reporter Kim Severson gave the Chick-fil-A bashers a coveted Sunday A-section megaphone, repeatedly parroting the "Chick-fil-A is anti-gay" slur and raising fears of "evangelical Christianity's muscle flexing" with only the thinnest veneer of journalistic objectivity. Severson, you see, is an openly gay advocate of same-sex-marriage equality herself.

Progressive groups are gloating over Chick-fil-A's public-relations problems exacerbated by the nation's politicizing newspaper of record. This is not because they care about winning hearts and minds over gay rights or marriage policy, but because their core objective is to marginalize political opponents and chill Christian philanthropy and activism. The fearsome "muscle flexing" isn't being done by innocent job-creators selling chicken sandwiches and waffle fries. It's being done by the hysterical bullies trying to drive them off of college grounds and out of their neighborhoods in the name of "human rights."

Remember, these were the same tactics the left-wing mob used in California to intimidate supporters of the Proposition 8 traditional-marriage initiative. Individual donors were put on an "Anti-Gay Black List." Fist-wielding protesters besieged businesses that contributed money to the Prop 8 campaign. The artistic director of the California Musical Theatre was forced to resign over his $1,000 donation.

Message: Associate with the wrong political cause and you will pay. So much for national "civility."

Interestingly, I don't think Islam is real big on gays right either, but I haven't heard much about those hateful blogs ragging on the Muslims.

The mainstream interpretation of Qur'anic verses and Hadith condemns homosexuality and cross-dressing.

Huh…cross-dressing? Who knew…? And was it a big problem before they condemned it?

SLIPPING AWAY...

If you are culturally aware enough to know what a "muffin top" and a "body shot" are (and incidentally, if you don't have time to master all these exciting new trends, these two can be combined into one convenient "muffin shot"), you may not think of them as being the most pressing concerns as our Republic sinks beneath its multi-trillion dollar debt burden. But, even if our economic and national security challenges disappeared overnight, we would still have to climb out of the cultural abyss into which we have tumbled.

I'm a great believer that culture trumps economics. Every time the government in Athens calls up the Germans and says, we've burned through the last bailout, time for the next one, Angela Merkel understands all too well that the real problem in Greece is not the Greek finances but the Greek people. Even somnolent liberal columnists grasp this: A recent Thomas Friedman column in the New York Times was headlined, "Can Greeks Become Germans?" I think we all know the answer to that. All societies eventually wind up with whatever financial situation the government and its constituency create in their mutually embraced, self-serving pact. So think of our culture as one almighty muffin shot, with America as a giant navel filled with the cheap tequila of our rising debt and…no, wait, this metaphor's getting way out of hand.

These are difficult issues for social conservatives to write about. When we venture into this terrain, we're invariably dismissed as uptight squares that can't get any action.

A few things that caught my attention on a recent visit to a local mall (but remember, I don't get out much): zombie teens texting, a thirty-something metro-sexual having his eyebrows threaded, a fifty-something cougar spilling out of her tube top, grade-schoolers in the latest "prostitot" fashions. And then there's the bigger picture: embarking on a lively tour of American's cultural levels, from schools to social media to churches to Hollywood. If there is a common theme in the assorted rubble of our cultural ruins, it's the urge to enter adolescence ever earlier and leave it later and later, if at all. So we have skanky 'tweens "dry humping" at middle-school dances, and an ever greater proportion of "men" in their thirties living at home with their parents.

Adolescence, like retirement, is an invention of the modern age. If the extension of retirement into a multi-decade, government-funded vacation is largely a function of increased life expectancy, the prolongation of adolescence seems to derive from the bleak fact that, without an efficient societal conveyor belt to move one on, it appears to be the default setting of huge swathes of humanity. It was striking, during the Hurricane Irene frenzy, to hear the Federal Emergency Management Agency refer to itself repeatedly as "the federal family." If Big Government is a "family," with the bureaucracy as its parents, why be surprised that the citizens are content to live as eternal adolescents?

Perhaps one of the saddest parts of America's cultural decay can be found in a brisk tour of recent romantic ballads.

Exhibit A, lyrics from a song by Enrique Iglesias: "Please excuse me, I don't mean to be rude, but tonight I'm f**king you..."

There are many more examples of where some of our music is heading, but there is no need to belabor the point. It's not the vulgarity or the crassness or even the grunting, moronic ugliness, but something more basic, the absence of tenderness. A song such as "It Had To Be You" or "The Way You Look Tonight" pre-supposes certain courtship rituals. If a society no longer has those, it's not surprising that it can no longer produce songs to embody them. After all, a great love ballad is, to a certain extent, aspirational; you hope to have a love worthy of such a song. But a number like "Enrique Iglesias' song" is enough to make you question whether the fundamental things really do apply as time goes by.

"The Radetzky March," by Joseph Roth, is a melancholy portrait of the decline of the Habsburg Empire seen through the eyes of three generations of minor nobility and imperial civil servants in the years before the Great War swept away an entire world order and its assumptions of permanence. Roth was a man of the post-war era, yet he could not write his story without an instinctive respect for the lost rituals of a doomed world. The novel takes its title from the great Strauss March that the town's band played in front of the District Commissioner's home every Sunday. As much as the Habsburgs, we are also invested in the illusions of permanence, and perhaps one day it will fall to someone to write a bittersweet novel about the final years of our Republic. But we will not be able to enjoy the consolation of a Strauss March. It just wouldn't have quite the same ring if you called the book, "F**king You."

To be 70...

I n 1960, after the Pittsburgh Pirates defeated the New York Yankees in an electrifying seven-game World Series, the Yankees fired manager Casey Stengel, who had turned 70 in July. The Yankees said he was too old. He said, "I'll never make the mistake of turning 70 again."

It is, however, a coveted mistake, considering the alternative, and remembering how recently it was that passing this milestone became unremarkable. The Bible, with the thumping certitude for which it is famous and sometimes tiresome, asserts that "the days of our years are threescore years and ten." If so, after turning 70, one has, ever after, the pleasure of playing, as it were, with house money. For what, exactly, would one now give up Mexican food and Bud-Light...longnecks?

To be 70 is to have escaped the disagreeable fate of dying young. But the Bible, which is replete with redundant reminders that life is real, life is earnest, adds this: "And if by reason of strength they be fourscore years, yet is their strength, labor and sorrow, for it is soon cut off, and we fly away."

To be 70 is to have seen the nation put away the almost casual cruelty of racial segregation. And to have seen, in the emancipation, not too strong a term...of women, and in many other improvements, how this uniquely self-transforming nation decided to declare unthinkable many practices that not long ago were performed unthinkingly.

To be 70 is to have been born shortly before Pearl Harbor, to have lived through the war that was already then raging, and the Cold War, and to have arrived at the sunny uplands of today. Yes, of course, man is still, and ever will be, born unto trouble, as the sparks fly upward. But never before in the human story has the risk of death by violence been smaller for such a large portion of humanity.

To be 70 is to have been born about the time competent medicine was born, with the arrival of penicillin, antibiotics and sulfa drugs. This is a reminder that contemporary America's most pressing domestic problem is a consequence of success. The crisis, the obsolescence... of the previous century's welfare state is a result of the social triumph represented by something unimagined 70 years ago, an enormous and expanding cohort of octogenarians.

To be 70 is to appreciate Mark Twain's example of aging vigorously: "I am able to say that while I am not ruggedly well, I am not ill enough to excite an undertaker." True, Twain had memory cramps of the sort that now are called "senior moments." He worried, "I'll forget the Lord's middle name some time, right in the midst of a storm, when I need all the help I can get." Nevertheless, he strode into the sunset wearing a snow-white suit.

To be 70 is to understand that time cannot wither, nor custom stale the infinite pleasure of simply trying to do things well, or witnessing others do them. Casey Stengel returned from exile to manage the 1962 New York Mets, an expansion team that, en route to losing 120 games, caused him to look down the dugout and ask in wonderment, "Can't anybody here play this game?" Few can, which is why the especially talented few...athletes, writers, musicians, thinkers, delight the many.

To be 70 is to experience a temptation generally worth resisting...the itch to natter on as Polonius did when belaboring Laertes with bromides. But to be 70 is to be running short on time for the pleasure of succumbing to temptations, so: Happiness, herewith the distilled essence of 70 years of experience...is a talent, and one that, unlike hitting a curveball, anyone can develop. Considering that America exists to protect the individual's pursuit of it, this pursuit is a pleasant duty.

Finally, to be 70 is to have lived 30 percent of the life of this nation, which is almost enough time to begin to fully appreciate the inestimable privilege of being a legatee of those who first unfurled the republic's sails and steered it toward the present. That is why, with homage to Frances Scott Fitzgerald...as we beat on, boats against the current, we should be borne back ceaselessly into the American past. It is impossible for the young to know, but never too late to learn, that America truly is something, perhaps the only thing...commensurate with our capacity for wonderment.

"Sometimes being lost, is so close too being found...and I find logic in that."

About the Author:
Richard McKenzie Neal

One should never equate education and/or intelligence to wisdom...

Richard was born in Hope, Arkansas (Bill Clinton's boyhood home), in 1941 and his father was gone prior to Richard turning two years old. He never knew the man, but attended his funeral as a sixteen-year-old.

Before boarding a Greyhound bus for California, at seventeen, Richard knew two stepfathers and a number of others who were just passing through. During those teen years, before succumbing to the beckoning allure of the outside world, Richard worked at an assortment of low-paying jobs. Summers were spent in the fields... picking cotton and/or watermelons and baling hay. He also worked as a plumber's helper and a carhop at the local drive-in burger stand.

After dropping out of school, eloping and landing in California, he soon realized how far out of his element he had ventured. And without the guidance of his "Constant Companion," Richard would have spent a lifetime floundering in a sea of ignorance and ineptness...and his books would not exist.

Richard's first book (Fridays With Landon) was driven by his son's life-altering heroin addiction. He had hoped not to author a sequel, but left the book open-ended due to historical concerns, which did in fact...resurface. For 25 years the family has endured the emotional highs and lows associated with the chaotic, frustrating and more often than not...heartbreaking task of rescuing one of their own, from the always ebbing and flowing tide of addiction.

The unintended sequel (The Path to Addiction...) was triggered by a mind-numbing relapse after 30 months of sobriety. The second book was then written to bring closure...one-way or the other. The author advanced several possible scenarios for the ending of that book, but only one of those possibilities was favorable.

His third book (The Long Road Home...) is a philosophical journey that we'll all experience as our time here begins to dwindle.

The fourth book (We the People) was driven by what he saw as the dismantling of America and the circumventing of its Constitution. Additionally, the ominous cloud of socialism and a New World Order looming over Washington motivated him to speak up, in spite of political correctness' muzzle.

This, the fifth book was written to confirm and document the realities of those fears and concerns chronicled in the preceding book. While those fears and concerns were driven by the current administration, his nightmare now is the possibility of that same administration being returned to office, for another four years, in 2012. He has grave apprehension regarding America's future should the unthinkable happen.

All five books were written after retiring from a rewarding, thirty-six years in the oil industry.

Our success should be measured by what we gave up (what it cost us) to obtain it...and not by what we accomplished and/or accumulated.

Richard McKenzie Neal

Vancouver Island

Contributors:

Victoria Davis

Landon A. Neal

Graphical assistance with book's back cover.

www.ingramcontent.com/pod-product-compliance
Lightning Source LLC
Chambersburg PA
CBHW061336280526
45784CB00001B/38